Letters from Alaska

John Muir, about 45. Courtesy of the Bancroft Library, University of California, Berkeley.

John Muir

Letters from Alaska

*Edited by Robert Engberg
and Bruce Merrell*

University of Alaska Press
Fairbanks

Paperback edition 2009 by
University of Alaska Press
P.O. Box 756240
Fairbanks, AK 99775-6240
Reprinted by arrangement with the University of Wisconsin Press

ISBN 978-1-60223-055-2

Library of Congress Cataloging-in-Publication Data

Muir, John, 1838-1914.
  Letters from Alaska / by John Muir ; edited by Robert Engberg and Bruce
Merrell.
    p. cm.
  Originally published: Madison, Wis. : University of Wisconsin Press, c1993.
  Includes bibliographical references and index.
  ISBN 978-1-60223-055-2 (pbk. : alk. paper)
  1. Muir, John, 1838–1914—Travel—Alaska. 2. Alaska—Description and
travel. 3. Conservationists—United States—Biography. 4. Naturalists—
United States—Biography. I. Engberg, Robert, 1943– II. Merrell, Bruce.
III. Title.
  QH31.M9A3 2009
  917.9804'3—dc22
                            2009010249

Cover design by Dixon Jones, UAF Rasmuson Library Graphics. Engraving is
"The Stickeen Delta," from *A Woman's Trip to Alaska* by Septima M. Collins
(New York: Cassell Publishing, 1890).

This publication was printed on acid-free paper that meets the minimum re-
quirements for ANSI / NISO Z39.48–1992 (R2002) (Permanence of Paper).

Printed in the United States of America

The role played by the editors in this,

John Muir's book,

is dedicated to Brock and Catherine Engberg

and to

Tod and Doreen Merrell

Contents

Illustrations

Preface

This book is a collection of articles the naturalist John Muir wrote while exploring the wilderness of southeastern Alaska during the years 1879 and 1880. The letters first appeared in the San Francisco *Daily Evening Bulletin* and are here being republished for the first time in more than a century. These distinctive writings retain the freshness, immediacy, and candor that mark Muir's best publications. They are also rare accounts of southeastern Alaskan history, coming before those of Ivan Petroff, Walter Pierce, and Eliza Scidmore in describing a territory newly acquired but little known. Muir's reports on the region's Natives and missionaries, gold mines, towns, mountains, trees, glaciers, and wildlife, and above all his unique perspective, are welcome additions to this literature.

Muir invited a generation of Americans to discover the unfamiliar northern acquisition named Alaska. His letters describe early Fort Wrangel ("... a rough place, the roughest I ever saw ... oozy, angling, wrangling Wrangel"), Sitka, Sum Dum and Taku bays, Indian villages, gold mines, the coastal regions, and Glacier Bay. "Alaska is a good country to live in," he reported, "polar bear and iceberg stories notwithstanding."

Muir's letters are more than simple guidebooks or adventure stories. Behind every account is found Muir's *glacial gospel:* that wilderness ultimately provides a place for journeys of the spirit. It is why he loved the Alaskan wilderness and why he urged Americans to journey north. "Go," he said, "go and see."

R.E. and B.M.
San Diego and Anchorage

Acknowledgments

The editors' thanks go to Ronald Limbaugh, Archivist of the *John Muir Papers* at the University of the Pacific, and to his staff, for the many courtesies extended us over the years. We are also indebted to Dr. Michael Cohen, Southern Utah University, who thought this collection worthy, and to Dr. Donald Wesling, of John Muir College, UCSD, for his useful critique of this book's Introduction; and to Jan Blakeslee, for taking on the task of editing the editors' work and doing it gracefully and with good humor. My thanks to Millie Stanley, of Portage (Wisconsin), Mike Rivers, former Park Ranger at Glacier Bay National Park, and Yosemite naturalist Shirley Spencer. Staff members at the Bancroft Library and at the Northwest Special Collections of the University of Washington were helpful in supplying copies of illustrative material. Professor Paul Sheats, UCLA, inspired me to think more deeply about Muir's "glacial gospel." And love to Sherry Engberg, who alone knows what Muir studies mean to me.

R. E.

Thanks are due to Hall Young's granddaughters Margaret Hughes, June Dona, and Grace Webb, for sharing family memories and the wonderful, unknown John Muir letter. I also want to acknowledge Frank Buske, formerly of the University of Alaska Fairbanks, for introducing me to John Muir on microfilm; Pete and Claudia Martin, of Bend, Oregon, and Camp Denali, Alaska, who taught me about seeing wild Alaska; William R. Hunt, for encouragement and repeated warnings of the folly of neckties; Chris Wooley, for glimpses of Alaskan Native culture; my fellow librarians Dan Fleming, Anchorage Municipal Libraries, Diane

Brenner, Anchorage Museum of History and Art, Kay Shelton and India Spartz, Alaska State Library, and David Hales, University of Alaska Fairbanks, for years of professional and personal assistance. And finally, thanks to Sharon, Kirsten and Andrew Merrell for accepting their husband's and father's obsessions.

B. M.

Introduction

Glaciers move in tides.
So do mountains.
So do all things.
—John Muir

In the summer of 1879 John Muir stood near the railing of the little stern-wheeler *Cassiar* as it cruised through Alaska's southeastern waters. The passing scene amazed the passengers and several quizzed Muir about it:

"Is that a glacier down in that cañon? and is it all solid ice?
"How deep is it, think you? you say it flows.
"How can ice flow?
"And where does it come from?"

Muir explained to the tourists how the glaciers were formed from the packed snows of the distant mountains. Patiently, he pointed out how the "snouts" of the glaciers drop off huge chunks of ice, in a process he called "calving," to become the bergs seen drifting in the waters around the ship. The travelers evidently listened closely to his explanations of the astonishing scenery. A few called him "that wild Muir" on account of his unbounded enthusiasm for the scenes they were witnessing, whereas others addressed him simply as "Professor Muir" (an unexpected title for someone who had been forced to quit grammar school at age ten, and who later dropped out of college). Yet all sensed there was a personal connection between the naturalist and the great landscape before them, and so the designation "Professor" was not entirely off the mark. John Muir *was* their teacher that day, and for the rest of the ship's journey people looked to him as their mentor in the wilderness.[1] They found Muir's informal lectures striking, and continuing into this century many thousands of others have found inspiration in Muir's books and articles. There is something timeless in his message that the earth should be viewed with a passionate amazement.

Alaska had been purchased from Russia and added to the United States only 12 years before, and these passengers were some of the earliest tourists visiting the remote territory. They were also among the first to be inspired by John Muir, who at the time was a relatively unknown naturalist (the profession itself was novel) working part-time as a journalist for the San Francisco *Daily Evening Bulletin*. The areas of southeastern Alaska that Muir's letters describe, though seldom visited in Muir's time, are now highlights of many Alaskan Inside Passage cruises, and modern readers will welcome the chance to compare Muir's accounts with what can be seen today.

Behind these descriptions is Muir's own story of his awakening conservation ethic. Three years before these Alaska travels, Muir had unsuccessfully attempted to convince California lawmakers to stop clearcut logging in the higher Sierra Nevada ranges. He suggested this ban in an article he wrote for a California newspaper. The politicians ignored his advice and Muir, perhaps discouraged and surely at the time most interested in adventuring and learning, stopped his political involvement, happily returning once again to his explorations around California. We think his political conscience and political voice were awakened once again by his Alaska experiences (they would not be silenced until his death in 1914). These Alaskan letters were his first sustained attempts to introduce to his countrymen the very *wildest*, and therefore (he would insist) the very *finest*, of America's lands. Muir moved from poetry to politics during these years of his life, and the impulse to lead a solitary, reclusive life faded away in the uncultivated Alaskan landscapes. These trips to Alaska seem to have prepared him to step on the national stage, how-

---

1. Muir was pleased that his *Cassiar* "students" listened to his lessons with an "earnest, childish wonderment." This original version of his conversation appears in "Alaskan Glaciers," San Francisco *Daily Evening Bulletin*, Sept. 23, 1879, reprinted in this collection. A later version is found in Muir's *Travels in Alaska*, ed. William F. Badè (Boston: Houghton Mifflin Co., 1915), pp. 55–58.

ever reluctantly, to become the acknowledged leader of the American conservation movement. We think the letters underline the importance of *Alaska* as a basic influence on Muir's life and mind.

Muir's story begins in Scotland, where he was born in 1838 to Anne and Daniel Muir. Muir's father, a restless man, emigrated with his family to Wisconsin in 1849. John Muir spent his youth on his father's two farms, and it was then that his fascination with geology and glaciers seems first to have emerged. The Wisconsin landscape, itself sculpted by the glaciers some millennia before, served as his first American outdoor classroom. Ever imprinted by his surroundings, the young Muir developed a natural curiosity about the agent that had shaped his adopted landscape. When Muir and his father selected stones for the family's new house at Fountain Lake, John picked up several smooth rocks and helped to set them at the home's door. These glacially polished stones are all that remain of that small house, an obscure but distinct reminder that John Muir's life seemed destined from the beginnings to be touched by rocks, glaciers, and elements of the earth.

Muir spent his youth in what he claimed to have been the uneventful life of a farm boy. From 1861 to 1863 he spent three years at the University of Wisconsin. His course of study was without traditional plan. He studied the classics, read voraciously, was introduced to botany, and toyed with wooden contraptions, one of which (a six-foot high "desk clock") is still on display at the school. He seems to have enjoyed his college days immensely, notwithstanding the fact that many of his friends were going off to fight in the Civil War and that he would occasionally see the maimed bodies of soldiers at nearby Camp Randall hospital. His one culminating classroom experience seems to have occurred in the presence of Professor Ezra Carr, who opened up the field of science to Muir. It was Carr who taught Muir about the new glacial theories of Louis Agassiz, the Swiss geologist then teaching at Harvard. Muir read the Agassiz books, no doubt discussed them with Carr and others, and seems to have developed a pretty good understanding of the formation, movement, and extent of glaciers. His curiosity later led him to recognize the first "living glacier" in California's Sierra Nevada and was one stimulus driving him to visit Alaska. Indeed, his first book, *Studies in the Sierra*, was about the glaciers in California's mountains.

But before glacier studies, Muir tried his hand at working man's machines. He was good at it, successfully making broom handles in Canada and wagon wheels in Indianapolis, during the years 1864 to 1867, while employed as a machinist and general handyman. Saying goodbye to his family and friends, he set off on his own, his departure perhaps hastened by an eye injury suffered when working in Indianapolis. (He feared his sight might be "Closed forever on all God's beauty!")[2] Muir evidently had a notion to visit either the Amazon or California. Indeed, California became his final goal, but only after he nearly died from malaria while walking through the South. California promised a healthy, nourishing climate and was, moreover, the state containing the great "Yosemite Valley," a painting of which Muir had seen while recovering from the eye injury.

In 1868, Muir arrived in San Francisco and immediately set off with a friend to walk to Yosemite Valley. Here is where he enjoyed a time of private study in botany and glaciology and of the Sequoia. It is the most luminous part of his career and the portion that most intrigues his biographers and his readers. Here, also, is when his white-hot need to understand the world shaped his special perspectives. "Mr. Muir the Poet," is what his friends called him, although his published works of the period show him more often to be an accomplished if amateur scientist.

His nonpublic journal writings of the Yosemite years reveal a more introspective man. They display a person harmonized to the peaks and valleys; they show he led a *wild* life: fantastic, rambling, intemperate, sometimes reckless, but always consistent and notably sane in its respect for nature and nature's rights. Muir seemed to live out the natural existence that the Romantics and Thoreau and Emerson only imagined. This youthful Yosemite span has endeared him to countless Americans, who view him as a genuine American hero, and indirectly explains why his life in Alaska has received relatively little notice. It is not just that John Muir was courageous, or that his brave mountaineering feats brought him fame. Rather, he seems to have undergone the stages of development that societies require of their heroes. The Alaska travels that Muir reports in the letters of this book mark the final stage of that development, introducing both his message and himself to the American public.

2. Quoted in Linnie Marsh Wolfe, *Son of the Wilderness: The Life of John Muir* (New York: Alfred A. Knopf, 1945; reprinted Madison: University of Wisconsin Press, 1978), p. 104.

Seen in such a light, Muir's journeys from Scotland to Wisconsin, to Yosemite, and eventually to the Alaska wilds all seemingly prepared him for a final task.

That mission was to re-enter civilization and to bring together the various groups who thought American wilderness should be preserved. It would prove a difficult and discouraging duty. Among the primary needs of the conservation movement was to identify someone who could be more than simply its spokesperson. The conservationists required a national figure who could popularize the unpopular; who could hold together by sheer force of personality the diverse interest groups of its fledging organization. It needed a Master who had experienced wilderness, who loved it, who had come to understand its value. The movement, in part, *invented a legend* (Muir himself) because it required a mythology of its own to combat the grand business figures who dominated the nation's politics. Muir adopted this role, partly because he knew he must and partly because he knew he could.

The many stories written about Muir's wilderness exploits at the turn of the century usually presented him to be a man without fear or selfishness. (Indeed, there is much truth in this version of his life.) Muir was made into something of a national *icon* ("Muir" would become California's most designated place name) as books and articles celebrated his adventures, to a degree that often embarrassed and angered Muir himself. These stories, repeated even now, often described a Muir who seemingly was never cold in any of his wilderness travels; who was never hungry although he walked *weeks* with only crumbs of bread and a packet of tea; who was never lost and never lonely. His mountaineering exploits inspired thousands then, as they do today. Young backpackers and rock climbers continue to pursue their image of Muir's spartan mountaineering. Photo-books and calendars appear yearly with his aphorisms about Yosemite and beyond. "Muir lives" appeared next to a painted "crack" in the Yosemite Hetch Hetchy dam not too many years ago, the work of a zealous anti-dam artist. Perhaps a student sweatshirt sold at UC San Diego's John Muir College best and most directly proclaims Muir's continuing reputation: *Let There Be Muir*.

Throughout his career Muir censured those who claimed that he was uncommonly brave or notable. He thought that the wilderness experience was open to *all* people, and that it took no great feat of endurance to experience wilderness. By adopting a champion's rank he would have subordinated this essential message. So, we find Muir demanding the reputation of an ordinary life, guided as much by chance as by destiny or heroics—"Fate and Flowers," he called it. Even as he became the conservation movement's mentor during the 1890s, he remained reluctant to write about the life that had shaped its development. It took a man of no less fame than millionaire railroad tycoon Edward Harriman to convince Muir there was something distinctive about his own story, and that it deserved a telling. Even then, Muir left his autobiography incomplete, choosing rather to write books that consistently made himself a background character in his own adventures in nature.

Muir's reluctance to accept celebrity status is spotlighted by his own reaction to an event from his first Alaska trip of 1879. His friend and traveling companion, S. Hall Young, fell from a ledge as the pair was rushing to the top of Glenora Peak. Young dislocated both shoulders and became completely immobilized, wedged between boulders directly above a severe drop-off. Muir scrambled back down to find his friend. Night was approaching and Young, fearing the cold and possible shock, insisted he not be left alone. Muir set one of Young's shoulders, wrapped both tightly, and carried his friend back to the ship, stopping to build warming fires along the way and offering words of comfort and encouragement.

Young later devoted an entire chapter of a book to "The Rescue." Muir, however, remained absolutely silent about the feat for nearly thirty years. Only in 1910 did he think the story might be told. He wrote to Young, complaining:

> Did you see George Wharton James's article in the [March, 1905] *Craftsman*, published in Syracuse, N.Y.? Evidently he had heard your lecture, and his account is a wretched caricature of the whole adventure. Although I never intended taking any notice in my writings of this adventure, after reading James' account I made up my mind to tell the story as it really was, and have written it but have not published it. When published, if published at all, it will simply be as a little story of adventure told among other adventures and will not interfere with your account.[3]

---

3. Muir to Young, May 31, 1910 (original letter in possession of Hall Young's granddaughter, Margaret Hughes; used by permission). The letter is reprinted in full in the *John Muir Newsletter*, New Series, 1:2 (Spring 1991), pp. 5–6. The *Craftsman* article is anonymously written.

This ten-hour rescue of Young from Glenora Peak is therefore absent from the letters in this book; it is even described in Muir's Alaskan journal of 1879 with but four words: "A night of it."[4]

Muir objected to notoriety and fame, yet eventually did consent to be the nation's wilderness authority. It may well have been one of his most difficult decisions, and we think he only reluctantly settled on it. The role once accepted, however, was jealously maintained. We find him, for example, carefully defending his public image during the later parts of his career when he was Sierra Club leader and national spokesman for conservation, not only because he wished to safeguard his reputation—as might anyone—but also and primarily to protect his conservation efforts. Leadership of that cause meant that both the movement and his own character must remain untarnished. He is found, for example, adamantly denying a contemporary charge that he had once cut down trees while living in Yosemite in the 1870s. (In a bitter letter to an editor, Muir insisted they had been "felled by storms.") He thought that another story describing a rattlesnake attack on him was silly. (He had killed the snake but afterward felt bad, thinking it "deserved life.") Muir went to great lengths to insure that some early, personal letters to Mrs. Carr would not be published. George James had the set of letters and by 1910 was interested in publishing them. This original set may have contained references to Muir's feelings about Mrs. Carr, or perhaps towards his Yosemite employer's young wife, Elvira Hutchings. Aware of the danger that loose talk or unedited letters might have on reputations, Muir tried to get the batch returned. (They were eventually printed, but only after his death, and only after someone abridged them by scissoring out portions or entire pages.) If he were destined to be a public figure, he fought to be one on his own terms.

Leaving a private life to enter the public arena, however, took its toll on Muir. How he felt about taking up a career in the "lowlands," about being a farmer and having "defrauding" civic duties, about settling "down"—and we are quoting his terms—is illustrated by a meeting he had with Young in 1888. Young unexpectedly happened by Muir's Martinez, California, ranch. When he spied Young walking up the path to the house, Muir reportedly exclaimed,

4. The words "A night of it" are circled in pencil. See *John Muir Papers*, "Alaska Notebook 24," 00027, p. 59. For Young's spirited account of the adventure see his *Alaska Days with John Muir* (New York: Fleming H. Revell Co., 1915), pp. 37–56. Muir's more sober version appears in *Travels in Alaska*, pp. 50–55.

Ah! my friend. . . . You have come to take me on a canoe trip to the countries beyond—to Lituya and Yakutat bays and Prince William Sound; have you not? My weariness of this hum-drum, work-a-day life has grown so heavy it is like to crush me. I'm ready to break away and go with you whenever you say . . . . Why, look at me and take warning. I'm a horrible example. I, who have breathed the mountain air—who have really lived a life of freedom—condemned to penal servitude with these miserable little bald-heads! [Muir was holding up a bunch of cherries.] Boxing them up; putting them in prison! And for Money! Man! I'm like to die of the shame of it. Gin it were na for my bairnies I'd rin awa' frae a' this tribble an' hale ye back north wi' me.[5]

Subtract something for Young's habit for hyperbole and we get a reasonable picture of Muir's post-Alaska frame of mind. It is, of course, never easy to give up cherished pursuits, yet Muir would do exactly that in his later years, when he devoted time to creating Yosemite National Park, to beginning the Sierra Club, and to the famous battle over Yosemite's Hetch Hetchy Valley. This reluctant but absolute acceptance to become the Mentor of the Conservation Movement was John Muir's finest accomplishment.

We find the beginnings of this dimension of Muir's life during his trips to Alaska in 1879 and 1880, when on board the *Cassiar* and while traveling with Young and their Indian companions. It is a story implicit in each article he wrote describing his adventures, but perhaps best shown in the final letter he wrote to the *Bulletin* in 1880. Indian Joe, one of the canoe guides, one day tested a rifle by shooting down a passing gull. Muir felt the killing to have been completely unnecessary and mean-spirited, and he swiftly condemned the Indian in no uncertain terms. (Joe evidently had no intentions of eating the bird.) The Indian's swift retort, recorded by Muir, was that he had *learned such carelessness for life from the whites.* It was a revealing charge. The Indians, Muir began to see, were being corrupted by civilization. They were losing their culture. Even their religions were being challenged; indeed, Young the missionary and Muir were agents of that very change. How Muir felt about the Christianizing of the Indians is not fully clear. He was, himself, never precise about his own religion, other than to claim that everyone needed the Savior while at the same time remaining critical of conventional church

5. The conversation is recorded in S. Hall Young, *Alaska Days with John Muir,* pp. 206–7.

dogmas. But if Muir was ambivalent about his own religion, he was none-theless saddened to see the demise of the Indian culture. They were, he observed in his article, being "whiskied nearly out of existence." This final letter is suggestive also because the experiences it describes hint at how common events undergone in the very uncommon Alaska land-scape profoundly influenced John Muir's life. The Indian Joe episode is a fitting conclusion to this part of Muir's development, illustrating that Muir's trips to Alaska were voyages of self-discovery as well as grand travel adventures. Muir was coming fully to realize the fragile condi-tion of the *earth* and its *inhabitants,* and to sense that we cannot corrupt the one without endangering the other.

Muir met one of those fortunate events which, he believed, shaped his life while at a Sunday School Convention in Yosemite Valley. He chanced to meet there a churchman and Alaska booster named Sheldon Jackson. The clergyman had lectured about his Alaska missions, while Muir talked on Yosemite geology, "fortified with a background of diagrams . . . [and] dissenting from the [Josiah] Whitney theory of local subsidence. He humorously inquired where the little granite plug went to that fell out." [6] Muir had thought about visiting Alaska before meet-ing Jackson, his interest having been furthered by a contemporary arti-cle appearing in *Scribner's Monthly* entitled "The Stickeen River and Its Glaciers." (Muir was then writing for the magazine.) Earlier that sum-mer he had received a letter of introduction to the premier of British Columbia, that Muir had apparently requested from the sender. The letter was enclosed with wishes that "you and Mr. McGee will enjoy your visit to the Northern wilderness 'muchly,'" [7] implying that the trip must have been planned sometime before Muir's meeting with Jackson.

Muir was drawn northward by the promise of adventure, by the pros-pect of finding new glaciers to study, and (no doubt) because he had played out his California studies and felt it was time to explore new ground. To his friend Mrs. Carr he sent a hurried note: "Good-bye. I am going home, going to my summer in the snow and ice and forests

6. Quoted in Frank Buske, "John Muir's Alaska Experience," in Sally M. Miller, ed., *John Muir: Life and Legacy* (Stockton: University of the Pacific for the Holt-Atherton Pacific Center for Western Studies, 1985); in *Pacific Historian*, 29:2 & 3 (Summer/Fall 1985), p. 114.
7. G. S. Mackey to John Muir, June 2, 1879. *John Muir Papers*, 00848.

of the north coast. Will sail tomorrow at noon on the *Dakota* for Victoria and Olympia. May visit Alaska."[8]

The branch of geology, *glaciology*, that studies both present day and historic glaciers, is today fairly well known. But a century ago it was a new science, and an amateur like Muir could still make significant contributions. Muir, following Agassiz, believed that a single ice age had once covered nearly all the planet, and that its influence could be found nearly everywhere. In fact, geologists now know there were three or four distinct ice ages in the history of the planet. Until about 15,000 years ago, virtually all of southeast Alaska was covered by a blanket of ice up to one mile thick. Advancing or receding, the ice was never still, always pushing down on the land it covered. By comparing observations made by the first Europeans 250 years ago to those made by Muir during his travels and to measurements made recently, we know that most glaciers of Southeast Alaska have retreated. As the amount of ice has decreased, the land (relieved of so much weight) has rebounded. At the entrance of Glacier Bay, for example, the rate of uplift is more than an inch per year. Because of the dynamic nature of these glaciers, few of the glacial landmarks Muir describes look exactly the same today. The Baird Glacier, which Muir describes in one of his letters, no longer reaches the sea, while the nearby LeConte Glacier recently advanced 680 feet in 18 months. Taku Glacier, also described by Muir, can no longer be visited by large ships; and the mighty Muir Glacier in Glacier Bay National Park has receded many miles from its 1879 position.

There remains, of course, much for the modern visitor still to see, and Muir's century-old accounts can be viewed as a sort of historic guidebook. Many of the 200,000 ship-borne tourists who visit southeast Alaska each year follow the sea-routes of John Muir's canoe voyages. These modern ships and the state-owned ferries of the region contrast sharply with the modest red-cedar canoe which carried Muir and his Indian companions; one 800-foot ocean liner cruises the route with performers who change costumes twenty times a day (or so the company advertises.) So many large ships vie for permission to enter Glacier Bay during the summer that their numbers have been restricted to about one hundred for each summer, in order to protect the whales and other sea

8. See William Frederic Badè, ed., *Letters to a Friend: Written to Mrs. Ezra S. Carr, 1866–1879* (1915; reprinted Dunwoody, GA: Norman S. Berg, 1973), p. 193.

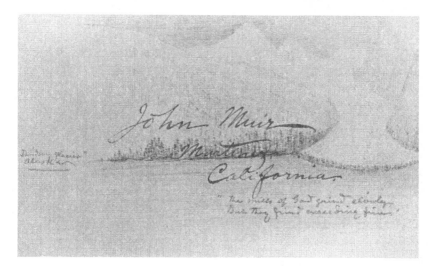

Davidson Glacier. Pencil drawing by John Muir, with his autograph. Reproduced with permission of the John Muir Center for Regional Studies at the University of the Pacific, Stockton, CA. Courtesy of the Holt-Atherton Department of Special Collections, University of the Pacific Libraries.

life of the Bay. Tracy Arm, the northern inlet of Holkham Bay (what Muir calls "Sum Dum Bay" in his letters) has had a growing number of visitors and is now on the itinerary of several tour companies.

It was the presence of these same glaciers that prompted Muir to travel to Alaska in 1879. Muir knew that the climate and precipitation of Alaska were ideal conditions for glacier building, and much of the glacial information Muir gives in these letters stands true today. But Muir's teachings about the great ice sheets were never mere scientific lecturing. They often became philosophic sermons about what he sometimes called his "glacial gospel," the belief that living in and studying nature would transform people. Such studies, he believed, had carved out for himself a truer relationship with the universe. It is noteworthy that Muir lamented that a favorite poet of his, Wordsworth, should have "died without knowledge of the glacial gospel." [9] Muir believed with evangelical passion that nature's glaciers could form men as well as mountains, and he might well

9. See Paul D. Sheats's discussion in "John Muir's Glacial Gospel," in Miller, ed., *John Muir: Life and Legacy*, pp. 42–53.

have viewed the proposed trip to Alaska to be a pilgrimage as much as a scientific expedition. In this way, his motivation may not have been so clearly distinct from that of the modern tourist who wishes to get away from it all by a visit to Alaskan wilderness.

The Alaska Appeal, *Vol. 1, No. 11 (August 30, 1879)*

Before he left on his first trip, Muir agreed to write a series of Alaskan letters for the San Francisco *Daily Evening Bulletin*, similar to those he had submitted earlier when he had traveled up and down California. Newly engaged to be married, and without steady employment, he knew the trip could provide royalties as well as adventures. (Biographers have placed Muir's departure on the very day after his engagement to Louie Strentzel, but we cannot find a clear date for the engagement. The diary of Louisiana Strentzel, Louie's mother, which is the only known primary source, has disappeared.) On June 20, 1879, Muir passed through the Golden Gate, a passenger on a steamship bound for Alaska. While still aboard he composed the first of the eighteen articles he would write that year and next. He mailed each completed piece back to the *Bulletin* by the monthly Alaskan supply ship, so the publication dates for his articles are several weeks behind their actual composition dates.

But if Muir was drawn north by the vision of Alaska land and its glaciers, he found himself, once there, almost as fascinated by its indigenous inhabitants—the remaining peoples of the Alaskan native Tlingit Indians. Numbering about 14,000 at the time the first Europeans contacted them, the Tlingits lived in territory that stretched over 400 miles along the Southeast Alaska coast, from modern-day Yakutat in the north to Dixon Entrance in the south. They lived in an environment that placed almost every material need within easy reach, and they enjoyed enough leisure time to develop a rich artistic and social culture. With the coming of Russians in the late 1700s, the Tlingits participated in the fur trade, later serving as middlemen between whites on the coast and the Athabaskan Indians of the interior. This role increased as the more easily hunted sea otters were driven to the brink of extinction in southeastern Alaska in the years after 1825.

By the time Muir arrived, the Tlingits' prosperous period was over. Disease and the sale of Alaska by Russia to the United States in 1867 had brought about drastic changes. Smallpox ravaged the northwest coast Indians in 1836 and left half as many Tlingits as there had been fifty years before. Other diseases followed, and the Stikine Tlingits who lived in the Fort Wrangel area were among those hardest hit.

The arrival of the Americans did little to better the Indian's problems. Americanization brought eager entrepreneurs. Sitka, the old Russian capital, boomed for one or two years after the Russians withdrew in 1867, but the boom was short-lived. Gold discoveries, up Canada's Stikine

River, were made in 1873, and caused the boom of Fort Wrangel, located opposite the mouth of the Stikine. This "Cassiar Rush" brought thousands of miners to the region, among them some 300 Chinese and 50 Blacks, many of whom spent their winters in Wrangel, enjoying the distractions of town life and returning once again to the up-river diggings each spring.

The U.S. Army—and later, the Navy—were given the absurd job of maintaining law and order over all this southeastern region. A few laws were effected, such as a ban on making, importing or selling liquor; but virtually no civil government was provided until 1884, five years after Muir's first visit. In this atmosphere of lawlessness and decline, the Tlingits soon learned the art of distilling moonshine liquor from molasses. Misunderstandings between whites and Tlingits were frequent and led to the burning and bombardment of several villages by the Navy. Squabbles between the Tlingits themselves led to Indian raids; in one such incident during the months between the two visits Muir describes in this collection, one of his Indian guides was shot to death on the steps of Young's mission.

Into this array of disorder and conquest came hundreds of gold miners. In time a few missionaries arrived. Russian Orthodox Christianity had made some small inroads with the Tlingits, but most of the Indians remained less than eager to compromise their traditional beliefs. The diseases, alcohol and general corrupting influences of the white miners finally brought a plea for spiritual help from one of the soldiers stationed at Fort Wrangel. It was the Presbyterians under Sheldon Jackson who responded first, in 1877. In a number of Muir's letters reprinted here, we read his reactions to these Christian efforts to save Indian souls. This was Muir's first contact with the Alaskan native American; his feelings toward them, at first sympathetic and condescending turned to respect in the course of his canoe voyages.

We have selected fourteen of these 1879–80 articles for reprinting in this volume. Some repetitive scenery descriptions have been removed; and in the interest of readability we chopped a few sentences with "bossy outcrops" and other crabbed expressions. We made paragraph breaks where none exist in the *Bulletin* accounts, either when these were obviously called for, or because they appear in Muir's journal versions. Where entire paragraphs were cut we have inserted a blank line. A deleted portion of a paragraph is marked with the ellipse notation "...".

Muir wrote his newspaper letters with several voices, including that of the scientist. While in that role he tended to list and catalog and describe at length, and the narrative results can be tedious. Perhaps because science marches on, with new terminology and discoveries, Muir's science correspondence is his least interesting. We have excluded some of these articles simply because their long descriptions of Alaska scenery add little to our understanding of Muir or Alaskan history. Otherwise the articles are complete as Muir wrote them, fresh and immediate. Muir wrote these articles in a style that probably mirrored his speaking manner, in a more unguarded and natural tone than are his later writings.

We have inserted one article into this collection that did not originally appear in the *Bulletin*, but was central to Muir's Alaskan experience—his 1879 "discovery" of Glacier Bay, first described in an 1891 travel brochure and reprinted two years later for the *American Geologist*. We have reprinted the account of the discovery that appears in the *Geologist*. [10]

We have preserved all portions of the letters that describe the various personalities Muir met along the way (Indians, missionaries, miners), including the lines on Samuel Young. The two first met when Muir arrived in Fort Wrangel. Young had spent the previous two years as the town's minister. (Fort Wrangel, with its one hundred "whites and Russians," five hundred Indians, and thousand or more miners from the Stikine River gold fields, was understandably considered fertile ground by the Presbyterian missionaries.) Muir and Young became immediate friends, as will be seen in this collection: Muir, the naturalist with a missionary's fervor; and Young, preacher with a naturalist's longing. Young thought they were the "most congenial companions," and wrote this sketch of his friend, the only primary description of Muir in Alaska that we have:

We both loved the same poets and could repeat, verse about, many poems of Tennyson, Keats, Shelley, and Burns. He took with him a volume of Thoreau, and I one of Emerson, and we enjoyed them together. I had my printed Bible with me, and he had his in his head—the result of a Scotch father's discipline. We had both lived clean lives and our conversation together was sweet and high, while we both had a sense of humor and a large fund of stories. But Muir's knowledge

10. The original article is found in "Alaska," *Alaska Via Northern Pacific R.R.* (St. Paul: Northern Pacific Railroad, 1891), pp. 3–17.

of Nature and his insight were so far beyond mine that, while I was organizer and commander of the [1879] expedition, he was my teacher and guide into the inner recesses and meanings of the islands, bays and mountains we explored together.[11]

Drafts of some letters found in Muir's journals closely resemble the articles as printed in the *Bulletin*, so we suspect that very few changes were made by the newspaper's editors beyond adding titles and subject headings. The paper evidently received several of Muir's letters at a time, a set coming down with the Alaskan steamers. These articles then were published serially, either in the order they were packaged or according to dates affixed by Muir. In either event, there was some confusion in the order of publication, and this we have corrected by matching the letters to Muir's known itinerary derived from his journals. The letters are chronologically presented in the order they were written, not in the sequence printed by the *Bulletin*.

In some cases, portions of a *Bulletin* letter appeared almost verbatim in Muir's posthumously published book *Travels in Alaska*. We have omitted many of those parts, noting such deletions in footnotes and giving suggestions about where to find the deleted writings. If we believed that the *Bulletin* version gives a different slant or insight, we included it; if there were doubts, we kept the piece, thinking it would add to both the integrity and the readability of the original letter. We have retained Muir's irregular spelling throughout, so the reader will find both *bowlder* and *boulder, cañon* and *canyon, Chilcat* and *Chilkat.* The editors have used modern spellings for their own words, including personal and place names, but have allowed Muir free rein with his.

Muir's *Travels in Alaska* was some twenty years in the making, and the final version was different from both his journal accounts and the ones that appear in this volume's collections. The book's history is of interest. It shows how carefully Muir constructed his manuscripts, and reveals the unfortunate consequence that the more he revised, the further he ventured from his most effective writing style. In 1894, Muir composed two notebooks based on his 1879–80 journals, thinking to use them when preparing his Alaska book. He did nothing with these notebooks, however, evidently too busy with Sierra Club and farm business. He set

11. Young, *Alaska Days with John Muir,* pp. 67–68.

them aside, and in 1910 returned to his original journals. "I also propose writing a book on Alaska," he wrote to Young in that year, "but that will not be before another year or so. The fact is that I have hardly commenced to draw upon my many note books and the results of my scientific studies have scarcely been touched as yet." Then, in 1913, the year before his death, someone prepared a copy of all his journal notes, which Muir then worked and reworked. In all there were 36 different versions of the Alaska manuscript prepared. One version lay next to him the night he died. The published edition of *Travels in Alaska* is from one of these 1913 versions.

The present collection permits Muir readers to enjoy, once again, his accounts of two wonderful voyages through a wilderness that has been forever changed. Historic Alaska comes alive in these pages: gold miners, rogue towns, natives, totems, even the infant tourist industry, become topics of Muir's interest. Throughout these writings we encounter his stylistic signature: the serene anthropomorphism and the very rhythms and rhymes that mark his prose. His descriptions let us imaginatively board the canoe with Young and the Indian guides to feel the roll of berg-waves and to enjoy the sight of a grand glacier "lying at home in its massive granite valley ... glowing in the early sunshine." With the *Cassiar*'s passengers, we too can hear Muir's explanations for the deep, blue crevasses and the thunder of calving ice.

The Trip of 1879

A Rough Passage

Muir's first letter from Alaska was composed five days into his trip, while he was still on board the Dakota. *Gazing out to sea, wistful about the mountain freedom he had exchanged for "the narrow bondage of a ship's deck," he recalled his decade of scrambling and sauntering, at his own pace, in the Sierra Nevada, while chafing at the inactivity imposed by the steamship. Traveling for his enjoyment, with no real commitments other than an occasional letter for the* Bulletin, *he was one of Alaska's first cruise-ship tourists.*

For Muir, the Dakota*'s cargo of seasick humans compared poorly with the free and graceful gulls pursuing her northward. Sighting several whales, he wished he could know them better. Before long, he would abandon the big ships for the more intimate possibilities of canoe travel.*

Muir's last glimpse of genteel civilization was in Victoria, British Columbia, with its solidly built businesses and cottages. Such scenes of domestic tranquility had an appeal to Muir, still a bachelor at age 41 (though newly engaged) and without a permanent home. He had said his farewells. "The world is all before me," he wrote his fiancée and her parents, paraphrasing Milton's Adam and Eve entering the unknown world outside the Garden of Eden.[1] The wilderness waiting for him in Alaska would overwhelm, captivate, and change him.

1. John Muir to the Strentzel family, June 25, 1879. *John Muir Papers*, 00855.

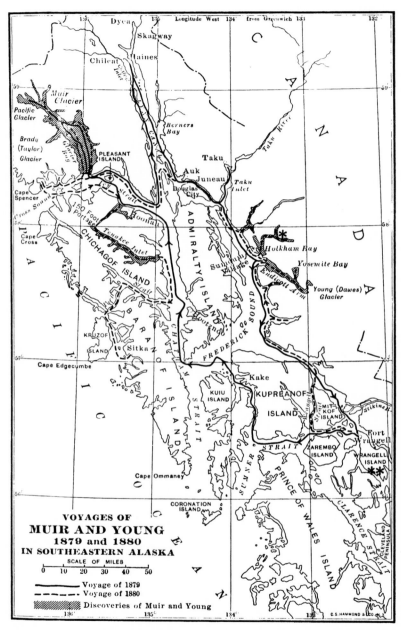

Voyages of Muir and Young, 1879–1880. From S. Hall Young, Alaska Days with John Muir *(New York: Fleming H. Revell Co., 1915). Places not shown on the original map, but mentioned in Muir's letters, are indicated by asterisks:* * Tracy Arm; ** Old Wrangel.

4

Victoria, V.I. [Vancouver Island], June 25, 1879[2]

C oming down from the mountains to the sea makes a grand change in the flow of one's life. For leafy woods, with their flowers and fruits, we have drifting tangle and dulse [kelp]; for granite domes, types of permanence, water-waves heaving in eternal earthquake, and the narrow bondage of a ship's deck for the wide freedom and wealth of the landscape. I left San Francisco last month on the steamer *Dakota*, in company with a friend, to see what I might learn in the new icy fields to the northward.[3]

After the usual flag-flying, public and private, on leaving the wharf was over, and we had sailed outside the Heads [Golden Gate], then the trouble and the enjoyments of the voyage fairly began. It was curious to note how suddenly the eager countenances of the passengers were darkened and subdued as soon as the good ship was free on the open sea and began to heave on the smooth swelling waves. The crowded deck was nearly deserted, and a dread gloom settled over all. The trouble was "only sea-sickness," the beginning of it; nevertheless, no funeral could show faces more deeply and truly gloom-clouded. First there was a going to bed, with a "this world is all a fleeting show" expression; then a staggering reappearance on deck to try to find out whether there might be any hope left in the fresh air; then a sudden introversion, intensely concentrated, as if every past act and experience were being passed along in mental review; then a rush to the rail and volcanic activity. The illness was so real, and the cause so natural and apparent, it seemed strange that nearly everyone afflicted should more or less be ashamed of it.

2. "Note of a Naturalist. A Rough Passage—Sea Sickness. Sea and Coast Scenery" appeared in the San Francisco *Daily Evening Bulletin*, Aug. 27, 1879, p. 4, col. 1. For further bibliographic information, see the "Note on Sources" at the end of this volume.

3. Muir actually left San Francisco June 20, 1879, the same month as the letter was composed; he made the same date error on the first page of *Travels in Alaska*. His traveling companion was J. Thomas Magee of San Francisco, a real estate agent and publisher of the *Real Estate Circular*, the magazine in which Muir had earlier published his call to halt logging and grazing in the high Sierra. Magee stayed with Muir only as far as Portland, when he returned home "for his wife—home—&—business." (J. M. to the Strentzel family, July 9, 1879, *John Muir Papers*, 00857).

Next morning a heavy wind was blowing, and the sea was corrugated with broad white-capped swells, across which the *Dakota* beat her way, head and stern up and down in admirable time, like a Spanish steer racing across a prairie. Few indeed of all our passengers were to be seen. The deck was about as clear and silent as if all had been washed overboard in the night.

How bare and poor a substitute for a summer landscape the ship made that morning! How poor a camp-ground. No wood or shelter, and too much water. Yet there is something extremely beautiful and exhilarating in the free sweep and swell of the dark heedless ocean. Long white tresses were streaming from the wave tops, and some of the outer fringes were borne away in the scud to wet the wind; and when the sun shone out it was brilliantly irised.

And how visibly was the skill and sufficiency of nature manifest in the gulls that followed us, skimming the rough waves against the wind in perfect strength and beauty, seemingly without effort, often flying near-ly half a mile without moving their long, narrow wings, swaying from side to side by simply tilting themselves this way or that, and tracing the curves of the waves with the finest precision, now and then grazing the highest swells with the tips of their pinions. How they can fly at the rate of ten or twelve miles an hour dead against the wind without a single wing beat is a mechanical problem not easily solved. How unlike the reeling, woebegone kings of the animal kingdom aboard ship, ill or half-nourished at a good table; they feeding in fresh, unchangeable health on the storm waves, their home, their resting place; when weary, some wind-beaten, surf-beaten rock. Well done for Nature in the matter of gull-making and keeping.

But here is still a grander and more striking revelation of brave warm life in the storm, created and maintained in the so-called howling waste—six whales, their great bulks appearing above the waves in near view like glaciated bosses of granite, each spouting lustily, then plung-ing down home in colossal strength and satisfaction.[4] Nor is this all, for together with and around the whales are a school of porpoises, a square mile of them, tossing themselves out of the waves in pure strength and hilarity, coming all the same way, keeping the ship company. A very storm of life, foaming in the waves and all moving as one. We cannot but feel

4. Most likely these were gray whales (*Eschrichtius robustus*).

glad to know that we have such neighbors in the unexplored wilderness of the sea. They are friends and fellow-citizens in the one harmonious commonwealth of the world, human like the rest of us, making a living as best they can and rejoicing in the good things provided them by the one All-Father.

Our ship, with its great iron heart beating on through calm and storm, is a burly, noble spectacle. But think of the hearts of these whales beating warm against the sea, through darkness and light, day and night, on and on for centuries. How the red life-blood must rush and gurgle in and out of their huge ventricles, bucketfuls, barrelfuls at a beat. One might well wish to come near these stupendous lives, but no close contact is allowed. We on land, they in the sea to fill and keep warm all the great world.

We arrived in the harbor of Esquimalt three miles from Victoria, on the evening of the fourth day, the harbor of Victoria being too narrow and difficult of access to a vessel the size of the *Dakota*. From Esquimalt to Victoria we made our way by a well-graded carriage road, which goes winding on through a charming undergrowth of spruce, oak, madrone, hazel, dogwood, alder, spiraea, willow and wild rose, and around many an upswelling, *moutonéed* rock, freshly glaciated,[5] and furred with yellow mosses and lichens. The town has a young, loose-jointed appearance, notwithstanding the importance claimed for it as the capital of British Columbia. It is said to contain about 6,000 inhabitants. The Government buildings and some of the business blocks are solidly built and quite imposing in bulk and architecture. The attention of the tourist will, however, be far more worthily attracted to the many neat cottage homes found here, embowered in the freshest and floweriest of climbing roses and honeysuckles conceivable. Californians may well be proud of their home roses, loading their sunny verandahs, climbing to the tops of the roofs and falling in bossy cascades over the gables. But here, with so copious a measure of warm moisture, distilling in dew and fog and gentle, bathing, laving rain, a still finer development is reached. And as to the English honeysuckle, it seems to have found here its very home of homes.

---

5. "Freshly" glaciated must be viewed in *geologic* time; no glaciers had passed through the region for some ten thousand years. The term *moutonée* refers to the rounded "sheep-back" appearance of mountains that have been overrun and eroded by glaciers.

To see what may be done in the rose and honeysuckle line is of itself a worthy cause of a trip to Victoria from the other side of the globe.

But still more interesting and significant to me are the glacial pheno-mena displayed here. All of this exuberant tree, bush and herbaceous vegetation is growing upon fresh moraine matter, scarce at all moved or in any way modified by the post-glacial agents. The town streets are graded in moraine material, among scratched and grooved rock-bosses, as unweathered and telling as those in the channel of the ancient *Mer de Glace* of the Tuolumne, 8,500 feet above sea level.[6] The harbor is plainly glacial in origin, eroded from the solid. The rock islets that rise here and there in it are unchanged *roches moutooce* [*moutonées*], and the very shores are grooved and scratched, and in every way as glacial in all their characteristics as those of a new-born glacier lake. That the dominion of the ocean is being slowly extended over the land by the incessant wearing away of the coast rocks, is well known, but in this northern, freshly-glaciated region the coast rocks have been so short a time exposed to wave-action that they are scarce at all wasted. The ex-tension of the sea, effected by its own action in post-glacial time in this region, is less than the millionth part of that effected by glacial action during the last glacial period. The direction of the flow of the ice-sheet to which all the phenomena hereabouts is due, was generally southward.

6. Muir is here referring to Muir Gorge, a valley formed by Yosemite's Tuolumne River.

Fort Wrangel, Alaska

A few days in Victoria and Muir was off to visit the Puget Sound area, arriving in Portland two weeks later for a quick visit and a descriptive letter about northwest scenery for the Bulletin *(not reprinted in this book).*[1] *He and a band of Presbyterian missionaries then boarded the steamship* California, *bound for Alaska, stopping at Victoria again and then at Nanaimo for coal. "Weather constant rain all day—a tepid, drizzling, leaf-making day . . . Leaving the [Departure] Bay, our trip to Alaska fairly began. I never before had scenery before me so hopelessly, over-abundantly beautiful of description. This enchanted land of lake and fiord, forest and waterfall, mountain and island, begins to appear in full force just below Departure Bay, and ends far north if it ends at all. It seems as if surely, following this shining way, we should finally reach heaven. What can the heart of man conceive more divine?"*[2]

Clearly, Muir was overwhelmed by the scale and scope of the wild country before him. For the first time, he saw in a single sweep of his eye countless first-growth forests "that have never yet been touched by the ax of the lumberman." The vista gave him an unforgettable benchmark against which to measure the poor condition of most California forests.

Muir's ship made several stops along the southeastern coast, but he remained on board, there being no suitable dry place to camp at the various stopovers. He sketched and made notes while the ship made its way to Sitka, its northernmost terminus. "Sitka has a rusty, decaying look—" he wrote to Louie, "a few stores, a few houses inhabited, many empty and rotten and falling down, a church of imposing size and architecture

1. "Notes of a Naturalist. John Muir on Puget Sound and Its Lovely Scenery. Forest Belts—Mount Ranier—Thriving Towns—Coal Fields. (Special Correspondence of the Bulletin) Seattle, Washington Territory, June 28, 1879." San Francisco *Daily Evening Bulletin*, Aug. 29, 1879, p. 1. Muir's journal notes of the voyage from Portland, dated July 10 through late July, 1879, are reprinted in Linnie Marsh Wolfe, ed., *John of the Mountains: The Unpublished Journals of John Muir* (Boston: Houghton Mifflin Co., 1938), pp. 246–75.

2. Wolfe, ed., *John of the Mountains*, p. 248.

Presbyterian Church and village of Fort Wrangell [Wrangel], Alaska. Courtesy of the Special Collections Division, University of Washington Libraries (negative UW 12068).

as if imported entire from Constantinople . . . cannon lying in the streets sinking like boulders in mud; dirty Indians loafing about."[3] Returning to Fort Wrangel on *July 14, Muir stepped ashore for his first close look at Alaska.*

Among the interested townspeople waiting on the wharf to greet the ship was S. Hall Young. Years later, Young recalled this first meeting with John Muir:

> *Standing a little apart from them [the other passengers] as the steamboat drew to the dock, his peering blue eyes already eagerly scanning the islands and mountains, was a lean, sinewy man of forty, with waving, reddish-brown hair and beard, and shoulders slightly stooped. He wore a Scotch cap and a long, gray tweed ulster. . . . He was introduced as Professor Muir, the Naturalist.*[4]

Muir was fascinated by the town, its people, its climate and promise. He determined to miss the steamer home and to remain in Fort Wrangel, to continue and expand his Alaskan studies.

3. Wolfe, ed., *John of the Mountains*, p. 259.
4. Young, *Alaska Days with John Muir*, p. 12.

Fort Wrangel, Alaska, August 8, 1879[5]

Wrangel Island is one of the thousands of picturesque bits of this cool end of the continent carved out of the solid ice of the glacial period—not by separate glaciers such as now load the maintain tops and flow, river-like, down the valleys, but by a broad, continuous ice-sheet that crawled slowly southward, unhalting through unnumbered seasons, and modeling the comparatively simple and featureless pre-glacial landscapes to the marvelous beauty and variety of the present day.

The island is about fourteen miles long, separated from the mainland by a narrow channel or fiord, and trending north and south in the direction of the flow of the ancient ice sheet. From the tops of its highest hill down to the water's edge all around it is densely planted with coniferous trees that never suffer thirst in all their long century lives, that never have been wasted by fire, and have never been touched by the ax of the lumberman. Abundance of snow keeps them fresh and lusty through the winter, abundance of rain and soft, shady clouds makes them grow luxuriantly through the summer, while the many warm days, half cloudy, half clear, and the little groups of pure sun-days, enable them to ripen their cones and perpetuate the species in surpassing strength and beauty.

The forests and the glaciers are the glory of Alaska, and it is not easy to keep my pen away from them. Nevertheless, I want to try to sketch this little far-away town and its people, and will gladly return to the trees and the ice some other time, after I have observed further.

Wrangel is a rough place, the roughest I ever saw. No wildcat mining hamlet in the grizzly gulches of California, or in the remote recesses of the sagebrush state [Nevada], approaches it in picturesque, devil-may-

5. "Notes of a Naturalist. John Muir in Alaska—Wrangel Island and its Picturesque Attractions," *Daily Evening Bulletin*, Sept. 6, 1879, p. 1, col. 4 [Reprinted Sept. 11, 1879]. Today Fort Wrangel is known as Wrangell, on Wrangell Island, in southern Alaska. This is not the island of the same name off the coast of Siberia, which Muir visited in 1881 and described in 21 later articles for the *Bulletin*, published as *The Cruise of the Corwin*, ed. William F. Badè (Boston: Houghton Mifflin Co., 1917).

care abandon.[6] It is a moist dragglement of unpretentious wooden huts and houses that go wrangling and angling along the boggy, curving shore of the bay for a mile or so, in the general form of the letter S, but without manifesting the slightest subordination to the points of the compass, or to building laws of any kind whatever. Stumps and logs block its two crowded streets, each stump and log, on account of the moist climate, moss-grown and grass-tufted on their tops, but muddy and decaying at the bottom and down their sides below the limit of the bog-line. The ground in general is a degraded bog, oozy and slimy, too thin to walk in, too thick to swim in. These picturesque obstructions, however, are not much in the way, for no wheels of wagon or carriage ever turn here. There is not a horse on the island, and but one cow. The domestic animals are represented by a few hogs of a breed well calculated to deepen and complicate and complete the mud, and a sheep or two, brought on the steamer for mutton.

Indians, mostly of the Stickeen [Stikine] tribe, occupy the two ends of the town; the whites, of whom there are perhaps about forty or fifty, the middle portion, opposite the wharf; but there is no determinate line of demarcation, the dwellings of the Indians being mostly as large and as solidly built of logs and planks as those of the whites.

The fort is a quadrangular stockade with a dozen block and frame buildings, located upon dry, rising ground just back of the business part of town. It was built shortly after the purchase of Alaska by our government, and was abandoned in 1872—reoccupied by the military in 1875, and finally abandoned and sold to private interests.[7]

6. In a letter to Louie, Muir continued his description of the rough town "a rickety falling scatterment of houses, dead and decomposing, set and sunken in a blacky oozy bog, the crooked trains of wooden huts wriggling along either side of the streets, obstructed by wolfish curs, hideous Indians, logs, stumps and erratic boulders, the mud between a little too thick to sail in and far too soft to walk in". (Buske, "John Muir's Alaska Experience," p. 115.)

7. The Russians founded the town in 1834 as Fort Dionysius, and it was renamed Fort Stikine in 1840 when the Hudson's Bay Company leased this part of Alaska. In 1867 U.S. Army troops arrived, and the name was changed to Fort Wrangel. The stockaded post of Fort Wrangel was built between 1868 and 1870 and sold in 1871 to trader William King Lear. Army troops returned in 1873 when the Cassiar gold rush began, and stayed until 1877. There is more about old Fort Wrangel in Clarence Andrews, *Wrangell and the Gold of the Cassiar* (Seattle: Luke Tinker, 1937).

Fort Wrangel, about 1879. Mount Muir is in the background. Courtesy of the Alaska State Library (photo no. 01-429).

In the fort and about it there are a few good, clean homes and people, golden nuggets of civilization which shine all the more brightly in their somber surroundings. The ground occupied by the fort, by being drained around the outside, is dry and wholesome, though formerly a portion of the general swamp; showing how easily the whole town could be made clean, at least as far as the ground is concerned. Were it removed as it is to the sunshine of California, with all its miry squalor, would it become a reeking center of pestilence? Here beneath shady clouds, and washed by cool rains and the fresh briny sea, it is ever safely salubrious. Although seeming to rest uneasily among mire and stumps, the houses squirming at all angles, as if they had been tossed and twisted by earthquake shocks, leaving but little more geometry in their relations to one another than may be observed among the moraine blocks of a glacier, yet Wrangel is a tranquil place—tranquil as the lovely bay and the islands outspread in front of it, or the deep evergreen woods behind it. I have never yet heard a noisy brawl among the people, nor a stormy wind in the streets, nor a clap of thunder, or anything like a storm-sound in the waves along the beach. At this summer season of the year the abundant rain comes straight down into the lush vegetation, steamy and tepid. The clouds are usually united filling all the sky, not racing along in threatening ranks suggesting energy of an overbearing destructive kind, but rather in the form of a bland, muffling, smothering, universal poultice. The cloudless days, too (which, by the way, are not half so rare in Alaska

Sheldon Jackson, from Jackson's book, Alaska, and Missions on the North Pacific Coast *(New York: Dodd, Mead, 1880). Courtesy of the Anchorage Museum of History and Art, Anchorage, AK.*

S. Hall Young. Reproduced with permission of the John Muir Center for Regional Studies at the University of the Pacific, Stockton, CA. Courtesy of the Holt-Atherton Department of Special Collections, University of the Pacific Libraries.

as seems to be generally guessed) are intensely calm, gray and brooding in tone, and inclining to Turkish meditation. The islands seem to float and drowse on the glassy waters, and in the woods not a leaf stirs. The air has an Indian-summerish haze along the horizon, and the same kind of brooding stillness, but is without the mellow autumn colors.

The very brightest of Wrangel days are not what Californians would call bright. The sunshine is always tempered in sifting down through the moist atmosphere, allowing no dazzling brilliancy—no dry, white glare. The town, like the wild landscape, rests beneath this hushing spell. On the longest days the sun rises about three o'clock, but it is daybreak at midnight. The cocks crow when they wake, without much reference to the dawn, for it is never dark. Cock-crowing is the one certain, invariable sound peculiar to civilization, but there are only a few, half a dozen or so all told, of full-grown roosters in Wrangel to awaken the town to give it Christian character. After sunrise a few smoke columns may be seen rising languidly to tell the first stir of the people. Then an Indian or two may be noticed here and there at the door of their big barn-like cabins, and a merchant getting ready for trade; but scarcely a sound is heard, only a muffled stir gradually deepening. There are only two white babies in town so far as I have seen, and as for the Indian babies, they wake and feed, and make no crying sign. Later you may hear the strokes of an ax on firewood and the croaking of a raven.

About eight or nine o'clock the town is awake and on its legs and in its boats. Indians, mostly women and children, begin to gather in scores on the front platforms of the half dozen stores, sitting carelessly on their blankets, every other face blackened hideously, a naked circle around the eyes, and perhaps a spot over each cheekbone and on the tip of the nose where the smut has been weathered off. Some of the little children are also blackened and none are overclad, their light and airy costume consisting of a calico shirt reaching only to the waist, as if even this flimsy material were sorely scanty, the whole weighing, when dry, about as much as a paper collar. Boys eight or ten years old often have an additional garment—a pair of castaway miner's overalls. These also are wide enough and ragged enough for extravagant ventilation. The larger girls and young women are quite brightly and extensively calicoed and wear jaunty straw hats, gorgeously ribboned, which glow among the blackened and blanketed old crones like scarlet tanagers in a flock of blackbirds.

Most of the women who load the store fronts can hardly be called loafers, for they have berries to sell, basketfuls of huckleberries, red and black, and of the large yellow salmonberries and bog raspberries, all looking fresh and clean, relieved most strikingly amid the surrounding squalor. They sit and wait purchasers until hungry, when, if they cannot sell them, they eat them and go to the hillside back of the town to gather more.

Yonder you see a canoe gliding out front the shore containing perhaps a man, woman and a child or two, all paddling in easy, natural rhythm. They are going to catch a fish, no difficult matter, and when this is done their day's work is done. Another party puts out to capture bits of driftwood, for it is easier to procure fuel this way than to drag it down from the woods through the bushes.

As the dozy day advances, there is quite a fleet of canoes along the shore, all fashioned after one pattern, high and long beak-like prows and sterns, and with lines as fine as those about the breast of a wild duck. What the mustang is to the Mexico *vaquero*, the canoe is to the Coast Indians. They skim along the glassy sheltered waters to fish and hunt and trade, or merely to visit their neighbors, for they have family pride remarkably developed, and are extremely sociable, meeting often to inquire after each other's health, to hold potlatches and dances, and to gossip concerning coming marriages, deaths, births, or the last murder, and how many blankets will be demanded as blood-money, etc. Others seem to sail for the pure pleasure of the thing, their canoe decorated with handfuls of the large purple epilobium [fireweed].

Yonder you may see a whole family, grandparents and all, making a direct course for some island or promontory five or six miles away. They are going to gather berries, as the baskets tell. I never before in all my travels, north or south, found so lavish an abundance of wild berries as here. The woods and meadows are full of them, both on the lowland and far up the mountains among the glaciers—huckleberries of many species, salmonberries, blackberries, raspberries, currants and gooseberries; with serviceberries in the opener places and cranberries in the bogs, sufficient for every bird, beast and human being in the Territory, and thousands of tons to spare. The huckleberries are specially abundant. A species that grows well up on the mountains is the best, the largest being nearly an inch in diameter and delicious in flavor. These grow on bushes about a foot high. The berries of the commonest species are a little smaller and covered with a bluish dusty bloom, and grow almost everywhere, on bushes from three to six or seven feet high. This is the species on which the Indians most depend, gathering them in large quantities and pressing them into cakes about an inch thick for winter use. The salmonberries are also preserved in the same way, after being beaten into a kind of paste, at least so I have been told. The species is quite generally distributed throughout the woods and along the stream-banks. I have seen some specimen berries measuring an inch or more in diameter. Delicious raspberries ripen around warm openings and rocky places, and along the edges of meadows and streams not too heavily shaded. Various gooseberries too, attain a fair size, and excel them in flavor. These last should be cultivated by those enthusiastic fruit growers who, with their thousand species and varieties already under cultivation, are still looking eagerly into the wilderness for more.

Most of the permanent residents are engaged in trade. Some little trade is carried on in fish and furs, but most of the business of the place, and its real life, is derived from the Cassiar gold fields, some two or three hundred miles inland, by way of the Stikine River. Two sternwheel steamers ply on the river between Wrangel and the head of navigation [Telegraph Creek, B.C.], 140 miles up, carrying freight and passengers and connecting with pack trains which make their way into the mining region over mountain trails.

These mines, placer diggings, were discovered in the year 1874. About 1800 persons are said to have passed through Wrangel this season for the mines, about one-half being Chinamen. Nearly one-third of the whole number set out from here in the month of February, traveling on the Stickeen River, which usually remains safely frozen until towards the end of April. The main body of the miners go up on the steamers in May and June.[8]

On account of the severity of the winter, all are compelled to leave the mines about the end of October. Perhaps two-thirds of all engaged pass the winter in Portland, Victoria and in the little towns on Puget Sound. The rest remain here, dozing away the long winter as best they can.

I want to say a line or two about the missionaries here, some of whom are devoting themselves to the Indians, while others seem to be devoting themselves to themselves. This letter, however, is already too long.[9]

The steamer *California* arrived this morning, bringing the monthly mail and a large quantity of freight for the mines and building material for a Presbyterian church in course of erection here. I had intended leav-

8. The Cassiar gold rush, one of many in the West, followed a familiar pattern: discovery by one or two prospectors, a rush of experienced miners, followed by the arrival of novices. From the beginning, there was also a steady presence of Chinese miners willing to work the white man's tailings. When Muir arrived in Fort Wrangel in 1879, the Cassiar rush was five years old and activity was declining.

9. Prudence may have kept Muir from continuing. As the next letter shows, the relationship between Muir and Sheldon Jackson, Henry Kendall, and A. L. Lindsley, officials of the Board of Missions, was cool. "The divines," Muir called them; in return, he was known as "that wild Muir." S. Hall Young, the resident missionary Muir met when disembarking at Fort Wrangel, would, however, share many of the adventures described in these articles.

ing Alaska for the present on her return trip [from Sitka], and spending the remainder of the season in Washington Territory and Oregon. But I have found so much to interest me in this noble wilderness, and so much kindness among the people, that I shall stay awhile longer and push back as far as I can into the mountains by any way that offers.

North from
Fort Wrangel

Southeast Alaska's only link with the outside world was the monthly mail steamer that had carried Muir north. Calling at Fort Wrangel and Sitka, and perhaps making a whistle-stop at a lumber or mining camp, the ship carried few passengers other than an occasional missionary and those with business of one kind or another. There were as yet few recreational travelers.

The gold deposits struck at Juneau in 1880 would bring more ships north, and more passengers and visitors.[1] However, it was a decade before regular boatloads of summer tourists made the journey north to "gawk at the midnight sun." By 1890, over 5,000 tourists were making the trip each season. Rival steamship companies competed for the trade, and railroad advertising brochures urged Americans northward.

Muir had a fellow publicist on board the Cassiar: the remarkable, energetic Sheldon Jackson, whose lecture on Alaska at the 1879 Sunday School Convention in Yosemite had so piqued Muir's interest in the Territory. With the twin goals of education and conversion to Christianity of Alaska's Native people, Jackson had first visited Alaska in 1877, spending the rest of his life promoting Alaskan interests. His deeds included the establishment of a school for Natives, in Sitka, and the introduction of domesticated reindeer from Siberia into Alaska, as a means of livelihood for the Eskimos. In a flood of letters, reports, books, and speeches he urged his readers to visit Alaska. His immediate, pressing reason for coming in 1879 was to help dedicate Alaska's first Presbyterian Church, in Fort Wrangel.

The curious boatload of tourists which Muir describes in the following letter consisted of Jackson, Kendall, Lindsley and their wives, S. Hall Young, and Wrangell

1. Muir himself was thought to be responsible for at least one Alaska gold rush. Badè believed Muir had directed Joe Juneau to a spot where gold would likely be found. This view was corrected by Frank Buske in his "John Muir and the Alaska Gold Rush," in Lawrence R. Murphy and Dan Collins, eds., *The World of John Muir* (Stockton: Holt-Atherton Pacific Center for Western Studies, 1981), pp. 37–49.

The Stickeen Delta. From Septima M. Collis, A Woman's Trip
to Alaska *(New York: Cassell Publishing Co., 1890).*

*trader John Vanderbilt (with whom Muir was staying,) and a mission teacher. The
shipboard party also included an interesting crew member. Robert Moran, age 22,
was the engineer on board, and was responsible for keeping up a head of steam.*[2]
Muir amusingly describes the conflicts between young Moran and the Cassiar's *Captain Lane.*

*Muir's long distaste for organized religion prejudiced his dealings with Jackson
and the other missionaries. (This bias had probably commenced when Muir's own
crusading father moved away to Canada to join a group of Disciples, leaving his wife
and John's younger sisters in Wisconsin.) Unfortunately for Muir, however, the limited
transportation options forced him to join up with the "divines" almost every time he
left his home base of Fort Wrangel. His abortive trip with them is the subject of this
and the next letter. Their destination was the Tlingit native villages at the north end
of Lynn Canal, near present day Haines. Chilkat, or Klukwan, was one of the largest
villages; its residents controlled important trade routes into the Yukon interior.*

2. Ten years later Moran was pioneering shipbuilding methods. Later he became a
millionaire and mayor of Seattle. His homestead in Puget Sound is now Moran State Park.

Fort Wrangel, Alaska, September 5, 1879[3]

Three Doctors of Divinity and a merchant and their wives, a lady from Oregon, a missionary and myself, made up a party to visit the fine wild glacial country of the Chilkats, 250 miles to the northwestward of here. We chartered the small sternwheel steamer *Cassiar*, usually plying on the Stickeen river, for this excursion, and had her all to ourselves. Under circumstances so extraordinary, everybody felt hopeful and important and rich—the poorer the richer—glaciers, mountains, a thousand islands, and officers to obey us, sailing and coming to anchor when and where we would.

The legitimate object of the divines was to ascertain the spiritual wants of the warlike and conservative Chilkat Indians, with a view to establishment of a church and a school in their principal village. The merchant and his party were bent on business and scenery, health and wealth; while I was moved by the glaciers that are said to come grandly down into the salt water at the head of Lynn Canal.

This was towards the end of July, in the middle of a block of the very brightest and best of Alaska summer weather, when the mountains, towering sublimely in the gray pearl sky, had rest from storms, and the islands seemed to float and drowse in the glassy, sunny waters, their green shores keeping them raw and bare. Furthermore, because these channels have all been eroded out of the solid by the glacier ice, and so short a time has elapsed since the ocean water was admitted, the small waves and ripples have not had time as yet to nibble away the shore lines to any appreciable extent. The glacial grooving and winding is still plainly seen on all the harder rocks, therefore the curves of the coast lines are, generally speaking, as finely drawn and unwasted as those of a living shell, and so under present conditions they will remain for thousands of years to come.

3. "Alaska Glaciers," San Francisco *Daily Evening Bulletin*, September 23, 1879, p. 4, col. 1. See also Wolfe, ed., *John of the Mountains*, pp. 262–66; and Muir's *Travels in Alaska*, pp. 56–62.

Were it not for the briny fragrance in the air, and the strip of brown algae seen at low tide, it would be difficult to realize that we are on waters in any direct way connected with the ocean. We seem rather to be on glacier lakes, thousands of feet up between mountain spurs.

After we had passed through the Wrangel Channel, the mainland, with its mountain range, came in full, clear view, adorned with crests and pinnacles, aspiring in most impressive combinations, and glaciers beneath of every form and size, some of the largest and most riverlike flowing down broad Yosemite valleys, their fountains far back and concealed, others plainly revealed, advertising themselves in open telling, mirrored in lines as keen and clear as those of a sheltered woodland lake.

This rare town, oozy, angling, wrangling Wrangel, with its comingled wealth of fish, furs, curs, Indians, traders, and all that, slowly vanished out of sight as we sailed past the north end of the island. The *Cassiar* engines, under the control of our economical engineer, wheezed and sighed with doleful solemnity, venting their black breath at wide, gasping intervals, suggesting the calamity that was so soon to fall. But we were happy then in the fresh morning and first love of our enterprise, and the barometer was too high for the sudden appearance of somber misgivings. Our course lay in a general northwesterly direction, through Wrangel Channel, Sanchoi Channel [Sukhoi or Dry Strait], Prince Frederic Sound [Frederick Sound], Chatham Strait, and Lynn Canal, all of which belong to that marvelously beautiful and involved maze of glacial fiords extending continuously northward along the coast from the Strait of Juan de Fuca.

Every island is forested to the summit save the largest, which rise here and there into snowy mountains, while the trees with a shaggy, leafy outer-fringe come close down to the tide line—the tallest underbrush frequently arching well out over deep water, so that one may sail in a canoe for miles beneath a luxuriant, arbored shade. For notwithstanding these long inland channels are at times swept by powerful storm-winds in the direction of their extension, no heavy swell-waves are raised to beat the shores and characters from top to bottom all along their courses. Every eye was turned to them and fixed.

Forgotten now were the souls of the Chilkats and the whole system of seminary and pulpit theology, while the word of God was being read in those majestic hieroglyphics blazoned along the edge of the sky. The earnest, childish wonderment with which this glorious page of Nature's book was contemplated was hopeful and reassuring. All evinced a commendable desire to learn it. "Is that a glacier," they asked, "down in the cañon? and is it all solid ice? How deep is it, think you? you say it flows. How can ice flow? And where does it come from?" From snow that is heaped up every winter on the mountains. "And how, then, is the snow transformed to ice? Are those masses we see in the hollows glaciers also? Are those bluish draggled masses hanging down from beneath the snowfield, what you call the snouts of the glaciers? What made the hollows that contain them? How long have they been there?" etc. While I answered as best I could, keeping up a running commentary on the subject in general, while busily engaged in sketching and noting my own observations, preaching the glacial gospel in a rambling way in season and out of season, while the *Cassiar*, slowly creeping along the coast, shifted our position so that the icy cañons were open to view and closed again in regular succession like the leaves of a book.

About the middle of the afternoon, we were directly opposite a noble group of glaciers some ten in number, flowing from a highly complicated chain of crater-like fountains, and guarded around their summits and well down their sides by black jagged peaks and cols and curving mural ridges. From each of the larger clutters of fountains a wide sheer-walled Yosemitic cañon opened down to the foot of the range, that is to the level of the sea. Three of the trunk glaciers flowing in these main cañon descended to within a few feet of the sea level. The largest of the three fed by eight or ten tributary glaciers, and probably about fifteen miles long, terminates in the midst of a magnificent Yosemite Valley in an imposing wall of ice about two miles long, and from three to five hundred feet high, forming a barrier across the Valley, extending from wall to wall. It was to this glacier that the ships of the Alaska Ice Company resorted for the ice they carried to San Francisco and the Sandwich Islands, and, I believe, also to China and Japan. They had only to sail up the deep fiord within a short distance of the snout, and drop anchor in the terminal moraine, and load to capital advantage.[4]

4. The glacier described is probably Baird Glacier, which empties into Thomas Bay. Muir's little history of ice gathering is an interesting and rare account of one of Alaska's earliest industries. From 1850 to about 1880, lakes near Sitka and Kodiak provided most

Islands, Sitidaka Bay, with fly. Journal page from Muir's 1879 trip to Alaska. Reproduced with permission of the John Muir Center for Regional Studies at the University of the Pacific, Stockton, CA. Courtesy of the Holt-Atherton Department of Special Collections, University of the Pacific Libraries.

Another, a few miles to the south of this one, receives two large tributaries about equal in size, and then flows on down a forested valley in a magnificent sweep to within a hundred feet or so of sea level. The third of this low-descending group is four or five miles farther south, and though less imposing than either of the two sketched above, is still a truly noble object, even as imperfectly seen from the channel, and would of itself be well worth a visit to Alaska to any lowlander so unfortunate as never to have seen a glacier.[5]

The boilers of our little steamer were not made with reference to using sea water, but it was hoped that fresh water would be found at available points along our course where the mountain streams leap down from

---

of this ice, which was sold in San Francisco for two cents per pound. Since glacier ice is made from compressed snow, it contains fresh water, even when scooped from the ocean. See E. L. Keithahn, "Alaska Ice, Inc.," in Morgan B. Sherwood, ed., *Alaska and Its History* (Seattle: University of Washington Press, 1967); and Terrence Cole, "The Ice Trade," *Alaskafest*, November 1979, pp. 34–35.

5. Probably Patterson and LeConte glaciers. The LeConte was named later for Muir's friend, geologist Joseph LeConte; it is the southernmost tidewater glacier on the West Coast.

the cliffs bounding the sheerest portions of the coast. In that particular, however, we failed under the existing management, and were compelled to use salt water an hour or two before reaching Cape Fanshaw, the supply of fifty tons bought in tanks from Wrangel having then given out. To make matters worse the Captain and engineer were not in good accord concerning the working of the engines. The Captain repeatedly called for more steam, which the engineer refused to furnish, keeping the pressure low, and running the engines at a ridiculously slow speed, for reasons known only to himself. At seven o'clock in the evening we had made only about seventy miles, a fact which caused great dissatisfaction, especially among the divines, who thereupon called a meeting in the cabin to consider what they had better do about it. In the discussions that followed much indignation and economy was brought to light. We had charted the boat for $60 per day, and the round trip was to have been made in four or five days. But at the present rate of speed it was found by means of a little simple arithmetic that the cost of the effort to reach and save the souls of the Chilkats would be from five to ten dollars too much for each person composing the party. Therefore, after considerable expenditure of fruitless negotiation with the purser, the majority ruled that we return next day to Wrangel, unsaved Indians, beautiful islands, sunny waters reflecting God, the grand glacial revelations and all, seeming in the midst of this solemn, deliberative financial assembly to have suddenly become mere dust in the balance. The Wrangel missionary [Young] was eager to go on for the sake of both the Indians and scenery, and of course so was I for the sake of the ice. It was easy, however, in the midst of our present abundance to bide our time. That slow engineer has much to answer for, and so also, I fear, have some of those halting doctors, because the Chilkats, while offering inflexible opposition to the advance of miners and explorers into their territory, have of late years been calling, like the ancient Macedonians, for Christian help. In turning back, though possibly influenced by some invisible necessity, yet nevertheless when they shall have returned to their comfortable feather-beds and parlors in the East, then in reflective moods surely some realization of a want in prosecuting the Lord's worldwork, some enduring sense of shortcoming that will not down, but rather rise gradually higher, like a glacial rock-boss in the very middle of their theological consciences.

Soon after the conclusion of this unhappy turn-tail discussion, we came to anchor in a beautiful bay [Hobart Bay?], and as the long northern day had still an hour or two of light to offer, I gladly embraced the opportunity to go ashore with Dr. Lindsley to see the rocks and plants. One of the Indians employed as a deck hand on the steamer landed us at the mouth of a bright singing stream. The tide was low, exposing a strip of shingly, shelly, dulsey beach, which sent up a fine fresh smell from its luxuriant growth of algae. The shingle was composed of slate, quartz and granite, named in the order of abundance. The first land plant we met was a tall grass, nine feet high, forming a waving meadow-like margin immediately in front of the dark, coniferous forest. Pushing my way through a tangle of bushes well back into the forest, I found it composed almost entirely of two spruces, *Abies menziesii*, and *A. Mertensia*, with a few specimens of yellow cypress.[6]

I was soon separated from my companion and left alone, and as the twilight began to fall I sat down on the mossy instep of a spruce. Not a bush or tree was moving, every leaf seemed hushed in deep brooding repose. One bird, a thrush, sang, silently lancing the silence with his cheery notes and making it all the more keenly felt, while the solemn monotone of the stream sifted through all the air, pervading every pore like the very voice of God, humanized, terrestrialized, and coming into one's heart as to a home prepared for it. How strange seem these untamed solitudes of the wild free bosom of the Alaska woods. Nevertheless they are found necessarily and eternally familiar. Go where we will, all over the world, we seem to have been there before.

Sauntering out to the beach I found four or five Indians getting water, with whom I returned aboard the steamer, thanking the Lord for so noble an addition to my life as was this one big glacial day.

6. In his edited versions of this letter Muir used their modern names: *Picea sitchensis* (Sitka spruce), *Tsuga heterophylla* (Western hemlock), and T. mertensiana (Mountain hemlock). The "yellow cypress" is *Chamaecyparis nootkatensis* (Alaska yellow cedar.)

Baird Glacier

The following letter, continuing the account of the abortive voyage of the Cassiar, *describes a trip to the Baird Glacier at the head of Thomas Bay and gives us some idea of what travel is like in recently glaciated country, where one is easily confused by the sizes and distances—the sheer magnitude—of the landscape. Today the face of the glacier is well over a mile from salt water.*

Fort Wrangel, Alaska Ter., Sept. 7, 1879[1]

O n the second morning of our broken-backed Chilkat excursion, everybody seemed cloudy and conscience-stricken, and ready to do any deed of redemption whatever, provided only that it would not cost much. It was not found difficult, therefore, to convince our repentant Captain and company that instead of creeping back to Wrangel direct we should make an exploratory branch-excursion to the largest of the three great glaciers noticed in my last letter. We had an Indian pilot aboard well acquainted with this portion of the coast, who, on hearing our wishes, declared himself willing to guide the new enterprise. The water in these channels is generally deep and safe, and though *roches moutonées* rise abruptly here and there at wide intervals, lacking only a few feet in height to enable them to take rank as islands, the flat-bottomed *Cassiar* draws but little more water than a duck, so that even the most timid raised no objections on this score. The cylinder-heads of our mysterious engines appeared to be the main source of danger to

1. "Alaska Glaciers: Graphic Description of the Yosemite of the Far Northwest," San Francisco *Daily Evening Bulletin*, September 27, 1879, p. 1, col. 1.

28

our devout company. Provided only they could be kept on, all might yet be well. But in this matter there was evidently some distrust of Providence, the engineer having imprudently informed some of the ladies that in consequence of using salt water in his frothing boilers, those iron heads might fly off at any moment, carrying softer heads with them. To the glacier, however, it was at length decided we should go.

Arriving opposite the mouth of the fiord into which it flows we steered straight inland between wooded shores surpassingly beautiful, and the grand glacier came into sight, lying at home in its massive granite valley, glowing in the sunshine, and extending a most noble invitation to come and see. After we were fairly between the two majestic mountain rocks that guard the gate of the fiord, the view that was unfolded fixed every eye in wondering admiration. No written words, however bonded together, can convey anything like an adequate conception of its sublime grandeur—the noble simplicity and the fineness of the sculpture of the wall; their magnificent proportions, their cascade, garden, and forest adornments; the placid water between them; the great white icewall

"Face of the great glacier, Stickeen River." From Sheldon Jackson, Alaska, and Missions on the North Pacific Coast *(New York: Dodd, Mead, 1880). Courtesy of the Anchorage Museum of History and Art, Anchorage, AK.*

stretching across the middle, and the snow-laden mountain peaks beyond. Still more impotent are words in telling the peculiar awe one experiences in entering these virgin mansions of the icy north, notwithstanding it is only the perfectly natural effect of simple and appreciable manifestations of the presence of God.

Standing in the gateway of this glorious temple, and regarding it only as a picture, its outlines may easily be traced. There is the water foreground of a pale, milky-blue color, from the suspended rock-mud issuing from beneath the grinding glacier, one smooth sheet sweeping back five or six miles like one of the lower reaches of a great river. At the head the water is bounded by a barrier wall of bluish-white ice, from five to six hundred feet high, a few mountain tops crowned with snow appearing beyond it. On either hand stretches a series of majestic granite rocks from three to four thousand feet high, in some places bare, in some forested, and all well patched with yellow-green chaparral and flowery gardens, especially about half-way up from the top to bottom, and the whole built together in a general, varied way into walls, like those of Yosemite Valley, extending far beyond the ice-barrier, one immense brow appearing beyond the other, while their bases are buried in the glacier.

This is, in fact, a Yosemite Valley in process of formation, the modeling and sculpture of the walls nearly completed and well planted, but no groves as yet, or gardens, or meadows, on the raw and unfinished bottom. It is as if the explorer, in entering the Merced Yosemite, should find the walls nearly in their present condition, trees and flowers in the warm nooks along the sunny portions of the moraine-covered brows, but the bottom of the valley still covered with water and beds of gravel and mud, and the grand trunk glacier that formed it, slowly melting and receding, but still filling the upper half, its jagged snout extending all the way across from the Three Brothers to a point below the Sentinel.[2]

Sailing directly up to the sunken brow of the terminal moraine, we then seemed to be separated from the glacier only by a low, tide-level strip of detritus, a hundred yards or so in width; but on so grand a scale are all the magnitudes of the main features of the valley that we afterwards found it to be a mile or more.[3]

2. Two landmark peaks on either side of California's Yosemite Valley, each standing some 3,000 feet above the valley floor and a mile apart.

3. This is a constant problem for viewers of freshly glaciated or alpine environment. In the absence of trees for reference, one's sense of scale is easily distorted. In the arctic, tourists may easily mistake a fox for a distant polar bear, or a ground squirrel for a grizzly.

The Captain ordered the Indians to get out the canoe and take as many of us ashore as wished to go, and accompany us to the glacier also, in case we should desire them to do so. Only three of the company, in the first place, availed themselves of this rare opportunity of meeting a grand glacier in the flesh—the missionary [Young], one of the doctors [Jackson], and myself. Paddling to the nearest and dryest looking portion of the moraine, we stepped ashore, but gladly wallowed back into the canoe; for the gray mineral mud, a paste made from fine mountain meal, and kept unstable by the tides, at once took us in, swallowing our feet foremost with becoming glacial deliberation. Our next attempt, made nearer the middle of the valley, was successful, and we soon found ourselves on good gravelly ground. I made haste in a direct line for the huge icewall, which seemed to recede as we approached. The only difficulty we met was a network of icy streams, at the largest of which we halted, not willing to get wet in fording. The Indian we had elected to go along with us promptly carried us over the difficulty on his back. When my turn came I told him I would ford, but he bowed his shoulders in so ludicrously persuasive a manner I thought I would try the queer mount, the only one of the kind I had enjoyed since gameday boyhood. Away staggered my perpendicular mule over the boulders and cobblestone into the brawling torrent. The sensations experienced were most novel and most unstable, but in spite of a dozen top-heaving predictions to the contrary, we crossed without a fall.

At length, after being ferried in this way over several of these outrushing glacial streams, we reached the glorious crystal wall, along which we passed, admiring its noble architecture, the play of light in the rifts and angles, and the structure of the ice as displayed in the less fractured sections, etc., finding fresh beauty and facts for study at every step. The Doctor soon left us to return to the boat, taking the Indian with him for portage purposes, while the missionary and I, by dint of patient zigzagging and doubling among the crevices and a vigorous use of our ax in cutting steps on the slopes and cliffs, made our way up over the snow and back a mile or so over the cascading brow to a height of about seven hundred feet above the base of the wall.

And here, too, one easily learns that the world, though made, is yet being made. That this is still the morning of creation. That mountains, long conceived, are now being born, brought to light by the glaciers, channels traced for rivers, basins hollowed for lakes. That moraine soil is being

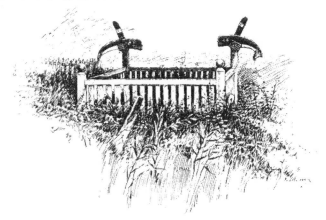

Indian graves, Sitka. From Septima Coolis, A Woman's Trip to Alaska.

ground and outspread for coming plants—coarse boulders and gravel for the forests—finer meal for grasses and flowers, while the finest, water-bolted portion of the grist, seen hastening far out to sea, is being stored away in the darkness, and builded, particle on particle, cementing and crystallizing, to make the mountains and valleys and plains of other land-scapes, which, like fluent, pulsing water, rise and fall, and pass on through the ages in endless rhythms and beauty.

We would gladly have remained on this rugged, living, savage old mill of God, and watched its work; but we had not bread, and the *Cassiar* was screaming nervously for our return. Therefore, threading our way back across the crevasses and down the blue cliffs in mean haste, we snatched a few flowers from a warm spot on the edge of the ice, plashed across the moraine streams without Indian ferry, and were paddled aboard, rejoicing in the possession of so blessed a day, and feeling that in very foundational truth we had been to church and had seen God.

An Abandoned
Indian Village

On the third and final day of the Cassiar *trip, Muir turned his attention away from nature and toward an abandoned Tlingit village south of Fort Wrangel. This account shows his deepening appreciation of Native culture, an insight missing from his earlier California writings. Like many observers of his time, Muir often characterized Indians as poor, lazy, and dirty. Yet when confronted with the evidence of the complex Tlingit culture in Old Wrangell's totems and ruins, Muir recognized immediately the Native people's rich heritage. He was particularly impressed with the Indians' involvement with nature and their subsequent natural enlightenment. His journal of July, 1879, notes as much: "the superstition in which all wild, or rather ignorant, peoples are sunk . . . [is] checked by more sound sense and natural reason than are found among the so-called enlightened and religious of our own race."[1] In Muir's view, Indians had their own good cause to deplore the dominating white culture.*

Some of the worst characteristics of that modern society were exemplified by the hypocritical missionary. Muir remained at odds with "the divines" with whom he traveled, and the following letter abounds with ironic and biting comment on the discrepancy of their missionary efforts. (Muir, or possibly others, tempered these frank remarks when editing this account for Travels in Alaska *many years later.) Muir's criticism became especially pointed while he was visiting Old Wrangell. This village, known as Old Town, Old Wrangell, or Kot-lit-an ("poplar tree town"), was the largest and best known of the early Indian villages in the Wrangell area. Located on a point due east of the Village Islands in Zimovia Strait, it was abandoned in the 1830s. Two events had likely contributed to its end and to the decline of similar Indian villages along the Pacific Coast: First, the Russian-American Company, which*

1. Wolfe, ed., *John of the Mountains*, pp. 273–74.

ruled Alaska, established a nearby trading post known as Fort Saint Dionysius (later Wrangell) in 1834; it is likely that Old Wrangell's inhabitants moved to be closer to this trading post. Secondly, a major smallpox epidemic in 1836 decimated native villages all along the coast of Alaska, and it did not spare Kot-lit-an.² Muir believed the old village's decay represented the decline of Alaska Natives; and, by extension, thought them symbolic of the fall of wildness too. These Alaska Natives and their historic totems, like humankind and the earth's trees, were quickly falling before civilization. "The Indians' only hope seems to lie," he concluded, "with good missionaries and teachers, who will stand between them and the degrading vices of civilization." Missionaries, however, remained, in Muir's view, problematic guardians—note his report, in this letter, of the Stikine chief Kadachan's eloquent objections to the white men's desecration of his family's old totem, objections brushed aside by the churchmen. (Kadachan's protest deserves a modern reading, and we included it here.) Read in its broader scope, this letter suggests the connections Muir saw between the fate of the Indian's totems and that of the planet; between the destiny of the Indians themselves and the fortune of all people; it suggests, too, his own calling as a wilderness missionary with influence to intercede on behalf of all.

Fort Wrangel, October 12, 1879³

Steaming solemnly down the coast after leaving the Great Glacier [Baird Glacier]—the cylinder head-heads still hanging well on their shoulders—the fair islands and mountains again passed in review to capital advantage. For the day was fine and the clouds that so often hide the mountain tops even in good weather were now floating

2. For more, see Robert T. Boyd, "Demographic History, 1774–1874," *Handbook of North American Indians*, vol. 7, *Northwest Coast* (Washington, D.C.: Smithsonian Institution, 1990), pp. 135–48; *Native Cemetery and Historic Sites of Southeast Alaska* (Juneau: Sealaska, 1975), pp. 110–11; and Ivan Petroff, *Population and Resources of Alaska* (Washington: D.C.: U.S. Government Printing Office, 1881).

3. "Wanderings in Alaska: A Lovely Sail—Majestic Mountain View," San Francisco *Daily Evening Bulletin*, Nov. 1, 1879, p. 1, col. 4. Two articles which appeared in the *Bulletin* prior to this one are not in this collection: "Alaska Coast Scenery" (*Bulletin*, Oct. 29, 1879) and "Alaska Forests" (*Bulletin*, Oct. 30, 1879). They are unexceptional descriptions of coastal scenes, parts of which were revised and placed in *Travels in Alaska*, pp. 13–18.

high above them, and scarce cast a perceptible shadow on the white fountains of the ice. So abundant and novel are the objects of interest hereabout that unless you are pursuing special studies it matters but little where you go, or how often to the same place. Wherever you chance to be always seems at the moment of all places the best; and you feel that there can be no happiness in this world or in any other for those who may not be happy here.

The bright hours were spent in making notes and sketches and in getting more of the landscape into memory. In particular a second calm view of the mountains made me raise my first estimate of their height. Some of them must be eight or nine thousand feet at the least.[4] Also, the glaciers now seemed larger and more numerous. I counted nearly a hundred of all sizes between a point ten or fifteen miles beyond Cape Fanshaw and the mouth of the Stickene River.

We made no more landings, however, that day, until we had passed through the Wrangel Narrows and dropped anchor for the night in a small sequestered bay. This was about sunset, but I eagerly seized the opportunity, small as it was, to go ashore in the canoe and see what I could of the noble woods. It is here only a step from the marine algae to terrestrial vegetation of almost tropical luxuriance. Parting the alders and huckleberry bushes, and the crooked stems of the prickly panax [devil's club], I made my way back to where the spruces were about a hundred feet high, from two to four feet in diameter, growing on comparatively open ground overspread with a continuous felt of mosses a foot thick. Here I lingered in the twilight doing nothing in particular, only listening to learn what birds or animals might be about, or gazing along the dusky aisles.

In the meantime another excursion was being invented, one of small size and price. We might have reached Wrangel this same evening instead of anchoring here, but were perhaps a little ashamed to show ourselves. Not because we had broken contract while breaking up the original expedition, or exposed ourselves in any way to the courts. There are no courts in Alaska, but there is conscience, and the *Cassiar*, and public opinion.[5] Looking away from the Chilkats, the owners of the *Cassiar*

4. The tallest Muir would have seen is Kates Needle, at slightly over 10,000 feet.
5. Purchased from Russia in 1867, Alaska was loosely governed by the Army and Navy—or not governed at all—for its first 17 years under the American flag. Civil government and the first appointed governor came to Alaska in 1884.

would thus receive only a $10 fare fare from each person, while they had incurred considerable expense in fitting up the boat for this special trip, and had treated us with marked kindness. No, under the circumstances, it would never do to return to Wrangel so meanly soon. This might hinder the Alaska missions, and cast everybody and the cause into the shadow.

It was decided therefore that we should grant the *Cassiar* company the benefit of another day's hire, and visit the old Stikine village fourteen miles to the south of Wrangel. This would be letting them and ourselves down at a respectable angle. "We will have a good time," one of the party said to me in a semi-apologetic tone, as if dimly recognizing the glacial wrong I had suffered. "We will probably find stone axes and other curiosities. Chief Kootachan[6] is going to guide us, and the other Indians aboard will dig for us, and then there are the old buildings and monuments." All right, I said in reply, it is all Chilcat to me. It seemed something grim, however, that so ponderous a mission of divines to the most warlike and most alive of all the Alaska tribes should end thus lightly in an official picnic curiosity trip to the dead Stickenes.

But divinity abounded nevertheless. The day at least was divine. There was plenty of free religion in the air, and about the islands amid which we now traced our way, and in the chaste sea-water, and dancing spangles. Sermons, too, in the glacier boulders on the beach where we landed, and how impressive was the ceremony of the baptism of the landscape in the drenching sun flood that day. The site of the old village is on an outswelling piece of ground sloping gently to the water. It is about 200 yards long, 50 wide, with a strip of gravel and a strip of tall grass in front, and the dark evergreen woods behind, and with charming views over the water among the islands. A perfectly delightful place to spend a life. The tide was low when we landed, and I noticed that the boulders along the beach, granite erratics that had been dropped by the ice during the glacial period, were piled in parallel rows at right angles to the shoreline, out of the way of the canoes that belonged to the village.[7]

Most of the party turned and sauntered on the gravel, for the ruins are overgrown with a tall tangle of nettles, epilobium, prickly rubus, elder

6. Kadachan (his name is inconsistently spelled throughout the articles) was a Stikine chief also related to the Chilkats. He was one of the four Stikines who accompanied Muir on his canoe trip to Glacier Bay later that fall.

7. Known as canoe runs, these cleared beaches were used by Southeast Alaska natives to pull their wooden dugouts above the high tide line.

bushes, etc., through which it is difficult to force a way. In company with the most eager of our relic-seekers and two Indians, I pushed back into one of the dilapidated dwellings. Not one in the village has its walls left standing. They were deserted some sixty or seventy years ago, and some of them are at least a hundred years old. So says our guide Kootachan, and his word is corroborated by the venerable aspect of the ruins. Nevertheless, though they are of wood, and the climate is so wet and destructive, many of the timbers are still in a good state of preservation, particularly those hewn from the yellow cypress, or cedar as it is called here.[8] The magnitude of these ruins and the excellency of the workmanship manifest in them, is perfectly astonishing as belonging to Indians. For example, the first we visited had been a dwelling about forty feet square, with walls built of planks two feet wide, six inches thick and forty feet long. The ridgepole of yellow cypress, still lying here in the damp weeds and perfectly sound, is two feet in diameter, forty feet long and round and true as if turned in a lathe; the nibble marks of the stone adzes are still visible, though crusted over with lichens in most places, giving it the appearance of stone. The pillars that supported the ridgepole are still standing in some of the ruins. They are all, as far as I observed, beautifully carved into a multitude of fishes, birds, men and various animals, such as the beaver, wolf or bear. Each plank had evidently been hewn out of a whole log, and must have required infinite deliberation as well as skill. Their geometrical truthfulness is most admirable. With the same tools not one skilled, civilized mechanic in a thousand would do as well. Few, indeed, could do so well with steel tools. Compared to this, the bravest work of our hardy backwoodsmen is feeble and bungling. There is a completeness about the form, finish and proportions of these timbers that suggests instinct of a wild and positive kind, like that which guides the woodpecker in drilling round holes, and the bee in making its cells.

But the most striking and openly interesting objects to be seen here are the carved monuments standing in front of the houses. The simplest of these consists of a smooth post, fifteen or twenty feet high, and about eighteen inches in diameter, with the figure of some animal on top, such as the bear or porpoise about life-size, or an eagle or raven three or four times as large as life. These are the totems of the families that occupied

8. Alaska yellow cedar, *Chamaecyparis nootkatensis*.

the houses in front of which they stand. Others support the figure of a man or woman, life-size or larger, usually in a sitting posture, and said to resemble the dead whose charred bones and ashes are contained in a cavity in the pillar made to receive them. Others consist of a massive pillar, thirty or forty feet high, the whole body of which is deeply carved from top to bottom into human figures, one above the other with their limbs grotesquely doubled and folded. In some instances the human forms are mixed with those of various animals and are said to have a mythological significance.

* * *

I was talking with an old Indian genius the other day, who pointed out one of the carvings he had made, and for which he told me he had received forty blankets, a gun, a canoe, and other articles, altogether worth about $170.[9]

Mr. Swan, who has contributed much information concerning the Indian tribes of our Northwest coast, mentions one specimen that cost $2,500.[10] They are always planted firmly in the ground. Most of these old ones, even, still stand fast, showing the erectness of the backbones of their builders.

While I was busy with my pencil I heard a chopping going on at the north end of the village, then a heavy thud, as if a dead tree had fallen. It appeared, that after digging about the old hearth in the first dwelling visited by us without finding anything of consequence, the archaeological doctor called away the Indians to one of the most interesting of the monuments and cut it down, sawed off the figure, a woman measuring three feet three inches across the shoulders, and conveyed it aboard the steamer, with a view to taking it on East to enrich some museum or other. This sacrilege came near causing trouble with the Indians, and would have cost dearly had it not chanced to belong to the Kootachan family, the representative of which is a member of the newly organized Wrangel Presbyterian Church. He looked very seriously into the face of the

9. For the deleted portions of the paragraph see *Travels in Alaska*, pp. 72–75.

10. James G. Swan (1818–1900), collector of customs at Port Townsend, Washington Territory, whom Muir had met on the journey north. Swan acquired a major collection of native artifacts for the Smithsonian Institution. See Lucile McDonald, *Swan Among the Indians: Life of James G. Swan* (Portland: Binford & Mort, 1972); and Douglas Cole, *Captured Heritage: The Scramble for Northwest Coast Artifacts* (Seattle: University of Washington Press, 1985).

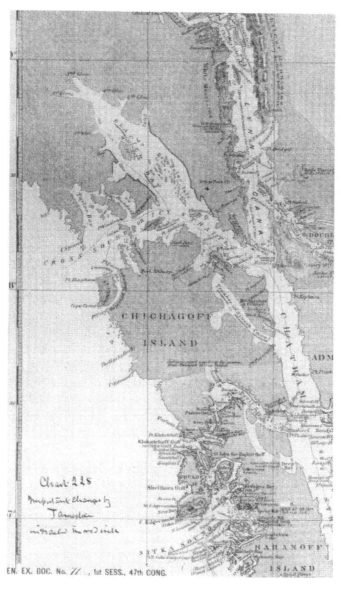

Muir's map of Glacier Bay, 1880, drawn from Captain L. A. Beardslee of the Jamestown. *Reports of Capt.
L. A. Beardslee, U.S. Navy Relative to Affairs in Alaska. In the Archives, Alaska and Polar Regions Department, University of Alaska, Fairbanks (acc. # RARE A0543).*

39

reverend doctor, and pushed home the pertinent question:" How would you like to have an Indian go to a graveyard and break down and carry away a monument belonging to your family?" However, a few trifling presents deeply embedded in deprecation served to hush and mend the matter, in consideration of the religious relations of the parties concerned.[11]

These noble ruins seem to foreshadow too surely the fate of the Stickene tribe. Contact with the whites has already reduced it more than one-half. It now numbers less than 800 persons, and the deaths at present greatly exceed the births. Will they perish utterly from the face of the earth? A few years will tell. Under the present conditions their only hope seems to lie in good missionaries and teachers, who will stand between them and the degrading vices of civilization and bestow what good they can. Thus a remnant may possibly be saved to gather fresh strength to grow up into the high place that they seem so fully capable of attaining.

Sometime in the afternoon the stream-whistle called us together. The sail to Wrangel was delightful. The water was smooth and gilded by a glorious sunset. The shadows of our sombre meditations among the ruins melted away. There was no trace of decay in the painted sky. Landing at dusk we pushed back through the midst of Indians gathered on the wharf, and across the low, crooked street up to our clean home in the fort, and thus ended the defunct expedition to Chilkat.

11. Jackson was also collecting artifacts, some for his alma mater, Princeton University, others for a museum he established in Sitka. Muir witnessed similar plunder of an Alaskan village near Ketchikan when returning south with the Harriman Expedition of 1899.

Southeast Alaska's Climate

Between the writing of the last article and the one reprinted here, Muir had taken a paddlewheel steamboat up the Stikine River with the missionaries. During this trip he had the memorable adventure with S. Hall Young on Glenora Peak. Muir then spent the next two months in and around Fort Wrangel, and returned to the upper Stikine for exploration and a second try at climbing Glenora Peak. [1]

To many, Alaska was a land of ice and snow, cold and dark, polar bears and igloos. By 1879 no gold or other mineral deposits of any significance had yet been located other than British Columbia's short-lived Cassiar rush; salmon canneries had just opened. Agriculture was non-existent. There were no lumber exports (only ice), and tourism was an industry only being anticipated. Why would anyone wish to spend good time and money visiting the frozen north wasteland of "Seward's Icebox"? [2]

Louie Strentzel's letter to Muir typifies the commonly held notions about Alaska: "and still another month of wondering in that wild Northland . . . I shiver with every thought of the dark cruel winter drifting down, down—and never a beam of sunshine on all that wide land of mists—what a blessed Thanksgiving if only you come home." [3]

Muir vowed to remain, writing to Louie, sometime in October: "Every summer my gains from God's wilds grow greater. This last seems the greatest of all. For the first few weeks I was so feverishly excited with the boundless exuberance of the woods and the wilderness, of great ice-floods, and the manifest scriptures of ice-sheet that

1. See *Travels in Alaska*, Chapters VI and VII.
2. William Henry Seward, Lincoln's and then Grant's Secretary of State, made the farsighted arrangement to purchase Alaska from Russia in 1867. It earned him much ridicule at the time.
3. Wolfe, *Son of the Wilderness, p. 209.*

*modeled the lovely archipelagoes along the coast, that I could hardly settle down to
the steady labor required in making any sort of Truth one's own. But I'm working
now, and feel unable to leave the field. Had a most glorious time of it among the
Stickeen glaciers, which in some shape or other will reach you."*[4] *So Muir would
remain in Alaska, postponing his return to Louie and the "defrauding duties of civilization." Meanwhile, and perhaps with an eye to soothe the upset spirits of Louie,
he composed the following short letter for the* Bulletin.

Fort Wrangel, October 16, 1879[5]

Alaska is a good country to live in, polar bear and iceberg stories
to the contrary notwithstanding. The climate of the islands and
of all that portion of the mainland that is bathed by the warm
ocean current from Japan, is remarkably bland and temperate, and free
from extremes of either heat or cold throughout the whole year. It is rainy
however, a wee hair too wet, as a Scotchman would say, so much so that
haymaking will hardly ever be extensively engaged in here, whatever
future developments may show among contemplated possibilities. But
even this rainy weather is of a good quality, gentle in its fall, filling the
fountains of the deep cool rivers, feeding the mosses and trees, and keeping the whole land fresh and fruitful; while anything more delightful
than the shining weather in the midst of the rain, or the great round sun-
days that occur in the months of June and July, may hardly be found
in any other portion of the world, north or south.

I never before saw so much rain fall with so little noise. There was
no loud rushing wind all summer, nor any thunder. At least I heard none,
and from what I can learn it is quite as rare a phenomenon here as in
any portion of California—a flash and clap, faint and far away, once
in two or three years. There is a fresh, sound, wholesomeness about

---

4. William Frederic Badè, *Life and Letters of John Muir*, 2 vols. (Boston: Houghton Mifflin Co., 1923–24), 2–126.

5. "Alaska Climate. Some Popular Errors Corrected. A Good Country to Live In,"
San Francisco *Daily Evening Bulletin*, Nov. 8, 1879, p. 1, col. 4.

even the wettest of this weather, that seems generally conducive to health. There is no mildew in the houses, as far as I have seen, or any tendency toward eternal mouldiness in any nook however hidden from the sun. And neither among the people or plants do we find that flabby, dropsical appearance which so soft and poultice-like an atmosphere might lead one to expect.

The most remarkable characteristic of this summer weather, even the brightest of it, is the palpable velvet softness of the atmosphere. On the mountains of California, throughout the greatest part of the year, the presence of an atmosphere is hardly recognized, and the thin, white, bodyless light of the morning comes to the peaks and glaciers as an unmixed spiritual essence, the most impressive of all the terrestrial manifestations of God. The most transparent and most brilliantly lighted of Alaskan atmospheres is always appreciably substantial, and oftentimes so thick that it would seem as if one might reach out and take a handful of it and examine its quality by rubbing it between the thumb and finger. I never before saw days so white and so full of subdued lustre.[6]

In winter, from what I can learn, the storms are mostly rain, at a temperature of thirty-five to forty degrees, and strong winds, which, when they sweep the channels lengthwise, lash them into waves and carry salt scud far into the woods. The long nights are then gloomy enough to most people, and the value of a snug home, with blazing, crackling, yellow cedar fire and book-covered tables may be finely appreciated.

Snow falls quite frequently, but never to any great depth or to lie long. Only once since the settlement of Fort Wrangel the ground was covered to a depth of four feet. The ordinary depth anywhere near sea-level is said to be a sloppy condition. The mercury seldom falls more than five or six degrees below the freezing point, unless the wind blows steadily from the mainland. Back from the coast, however, beyond the mountains, the winter months are intensely cold. At Glenora, on the Stickene River, less than a thousand feet above the level of the sea, a temperature of from thirty to forty degrees below zero is not uncommon.[7]

6. Mountain forests often look hazy in warm weather, partly because of naturally occurring hydrocarbons, known as terpenes, being released into the air; Muir's enthusiastic description may be of such a phenomenon.

7. Muir had been in Glenora just two weeks before, when he had had his mountain rescue adventure with Young.

Discovery of
Glacier Bay

"Leave for the North in a few minutes. Indians waiting. Farewell," Muir wrote to Louie on October 9, 1879.[1] *With his friend Young, the Indians Toyatte, Kadachan, Sitka Charley, and Stickeen John, Muir left Fort Wrangel in a thirty-five foot Indian* kladushu etlan *(red-cedar dugout) canoe. Their goal was to explore the southeastern waters of Alaska.*

The group "stored our baggage, which was not burdensome, in one end of the canoe, taking a simple store of provisions—flour, beans, bacon, sugar, salt and a little dried fruit," remembered Young in his book about the trip. "We did not get off without trouble. Kadachan's mother . . strongly objected to my taking her son on so perilous a voyage and so late in the season, and when her scoldings and entreaties did not avail she said, 'If anything happens to my son, I will take your baby as mine in payment'."[2]

It was a cold, windy, rainy time of year, a time when almost nobody travelled. The rain came so often during their trip that periods of sunshine brought shouts (said Muir) of "joyous acclamation." The group paddled and sailed northward through Summer Strait, north past Kupreanof Island, Frederick Sound, and up Chatham Strait. Young planned to "talk religion" to the Indians at the head of Lynn Canal, but rumors of a civil war among the Chilkats persuaded the group instead to turn west in search of "ice mountains." Their ultimate goal was a place Muir had heard mentioned while in Fort Wrangel. The Indians called it "Sita-da-ka."

Sailing when the winds were favorable, or else paddling, the group spent nights camped where fresh water was available. They stopped at several Indian villages where Young told the "Great New Story." One such village greeted the group with a hail of bullets. "Instinctively Muir and I ceased to paddle, but Tow-a-att commanded,

---

1. Wolfe, *Son of the Wilderness*, p. 209. Young wrote that they left on October 14.
2. Young, *Alaska Days with John Muir*, p. 70.

44

'Hut-ha, hut-ha!—*pull, pull' and slowly, amid the dropping bullets, we zigzagged our way up the channel."*

Evidently Muir would sometimes join Young in preaching to the Indians: "Muir told the eager natives wonderful things about what the great one God, whose name is Love, was doing for them."[3] *Around the campfires Muir listened to the Indians tell stories of the old days, and learned much of the Indians' culture. He gained an increased admiration for it, coming to believe that the Indians were closer to an "immanent living Principle in all matter" than were the "civilized exponents of Christianity."*[4]

Late in the day of October 23, they reached Hoonah, the main village of the Hoonah Tlingits. One Indian told Muir of a great bay to the northwest, adding that it was a deadly place filled with the dangerous spirit of Kooshta-kah, *the otter man. The group reached Pleasant Island on October 24, where they loaded wood for later fires. The Indians continued this far with Muir and Young in part because of their confidence in Young's God, and their belief that Muir, whom they called the "Great Ice Chief," could ward off dangers. Pushing on the next morning, unsure of their position, the group spotted a campfire across from Berg Bay and steered toward it. There they met a hunting party of Hoonahs. Muir learned that the large bay was the "Sita-da-ka" about which he had heard, and that many glaciers could be found bordering it. Muir hired a young seal hunter as a guide. He received a second warning. "It is my husband you are taking away," the man's wife told Muir. "See that you bring him back." The party continued up the Bay, first camping near Geikie Inlet. The next day was a Sunday and Young and the Indians preferred to stay in camp; Muir climbed alone up a nearby ridge. Here he caught his first view of Glacier Bay, jotting into his journal his first impressions: "a solitude of ice and snow and newborn rocks, dim, dreary, mysterious."*

Muir would return to this area in 1880 and report his findings to Captain Lester Anthony Beardslee of the U.S. Navy, in Sitka. Muir helped also to develop a map

3. For these incidents we use Young's version taken from his *Alaska Days with John Muir*, pp. 74–92. Nowhere does Muir mention the "bullets" incident.

4. In Wolfe, *Son of the Wilderness*, p. 209. The character of Muir's religion has been a subject of much interest to his biographers. Young called him a "devout theist." Others have held him to be influenced by Eastern thought and mysticism. Muir's status as an ethical Christian is admirably argued by Ronald Limbaugh, "The Nature of John Muir's Religion," in Miller, ed., *John Muir: Life and Legacy*, pp. 16–27; this argument is echoed by Richard C. Austin, *Baptized into Wilderness: A Christian Perspective of John Muir* (Atlanta: John Knox Press, 1987).

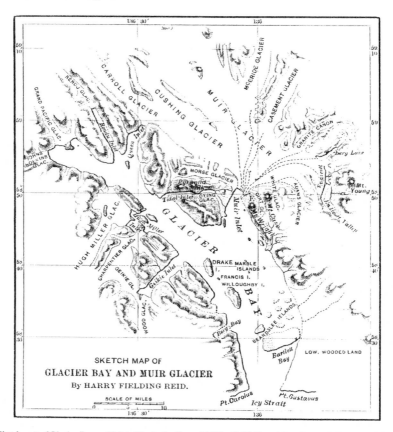

Sketch map of Glacier Bay and Muir Glacier by Harry Fielding Reid. From Eliza Ruhamah Scidmore, The Guide-Book to Alaska and the Northwest Coast *(London: William Heinemann, 1893).*

of the area. It was at this time that "Glacier Bay" was mapped and the name given to the area.[5] *The "Muir" title was given to the Bay's largest glacier, again by Beardslee, with perhaps Young advising. Muir was later mistakenly given credit for the discovery of Glacier Bay, largely because of the articles he wrote about this trip*

5. Lester Anthony Beardslee (1836–1903), USN, was in command of the U.S.S. *Jamestown*, sent to Sitka in 1879 because of the threat of an Indian revolt. Landmarks in Glacier Bay are named for him. For the map constructed with Muir's help, see William F. and Maymie B. Kimes, *John Muir: A Reading Bibliography* (Fresno: Panorama West Books, 1986), p. 38. For more on Beardslee, see Muir's letter of August 14, 1880, later in this volume.

(including the one we present here), but clearly one Charles Wood recorded the first visit to the Bay by a non-native in 1877.[6] *Muir wrote about his "Discovery" a dozen years later, in 1893, with the publication of the following article "Alaska."*

What follows is splendid adventure. Readers familiar with later versions, including that found in Travels in Alaska, *will enjoy this fresh, more immediate description of the days in "Sita-da-ka." We have preserved Muir's inconsistent spelling of the Indians' names (Charly, Charlie; Toyette, Toyatte) and of the geographic place names (Sita-da-ka, Stikeen, Glacier bay).*

"Alaska"[7]

I made my first visit to Glacier bay toward the end of October, 1879. Winter weather had set in; young ice was forming in the sheltered inlets, and the mountains had received a fresh covering of snow. It was then unexplored and unknown except to Indians. Vancouver, who surveyed the coast nearly a hundred years ago, missed it altogether, on account, I suppose, of bad weather and a jam of ice across its mouth.[8]

I had spent the best part of the season exploring the cañon of the Stikeen river, and a little of the interior region on the divide of some of the southerly tributaries of the Yukon and Mackenzie. It was getting rather late for new undertakings when I returned to Wrangel, but eagerness to see some of the glaciers to the northward, however imperfectly, drove me on. Assisted by Mr. Young, the enthusiastic Alaska missionary, I succeeded in procuring a canoe and a crew of four Indians—Toyette, Kadechan, Stikeen John, and Sitka Charly. Mr. Young, who is anxious to learn something of the numbers and condition of the Indian tribes

6. See the discussion in Dave Bohn, *Glacier Bay: The Land and the Silence* (Gustavus, AK: Alaska National Parks and Monuments Association, 1976), Chapter II.

7. *American Geologist*, 11:5 (May 1893), pp. 295–99. This is a slightly modified reprint of "Alaska," in *Alaska via Northern Pacific R.R.* (St. Paul: Northern Pacific Railroad, 1891), pp. 3–17. Only that portion dealing with Glacier Bay is reproduced here. An expanded version of the article, including his return trip of 1880 to Glacier Bay, appeared as "Discovery of Glacier Bay," *Century Magazine*, Vol. 50, No. 2 (June 1895), pp. 234–37.

8. Captain George Vancouver's map of 1794 shows only a small indentation where Glacier Bay is located.

that might be seen on the way, agreed to go with me. Hastily gathering the necessary supplies, we set forth October 14th. While we were on the west shore of Admiralty island, intending to make a direct course up Lynn canal, we learned that the Chilcat Indians were drinking and fighting, and that it would be unsafe to go among them until their quarrels were settled. I decided therefore to turn westward through Icy strait and go in search of Sitka Charly's wonderful "ice mountains." Charly, who was the youngest of my crew, having noticed my interest in glaciers, told me that when he was a boy he had gone with his father to hunt seals in a large bay full of ice, and he thought that he could find it.

On the 24th [October, 1879], as we approached an island in the middle of Icy strait, Charlie said that we must procure a supply of wood there to carry with us, because beyond this the country was bare of trees. Hitherto we had picked our way by Vancouver's chart, but now it failed us. Guided by Charlie, who alone knew anything of the region, we arrived late in what is now called "Bartlett bay," near the mouth of Glacier bay, where we made a cold camp in rain and snow and darkness. At daylight on the 25th we noticed a smoke, where we found a party of Hoonah seal-hunters huddled together in a small bark hut. Here Sitka Charlie seemed lost. He declared the place had changed so much he hardly recognized it, but I succeeded in hiring one of the hunters to go with us up the main Glacier bay, or "Sita-da-ka," as the Indians called it. The weather was stormy, cold rain fell fast, and low, dull clouds muffled the mountains, making the strange, treeless land all the more dreary and forbidding. About noon we passed the first of the low descending glaciers [Geikie Glacier] on the west side, and found a landing-place a few miles beyond it. While camp was being made I strolled along the shore, eagerly examining the fossil wood with which it was strewn, and watching for glimpses of the glaciers beneath the watery clouds. Next day the storm continued, a wild southeaster was howling over the icy wilderness, and everybody wished to remain in camp. Therefore I set out alone to see what I might learn. Pushing on through mud and sludgy snow I gained at length a commanding outlook on a bald promontory about 1,500 feet high. All the landscape was smothered in busy clouds, and I began to fear that I had climbed in vain, when at last the clouds lifted a little, and the ice-filled expanse of the bay, and the feet of the mountains that stand about it, and the imposing fronts of five of the great glaciers, were dis-

"View of Sitidaka Bay." From Muir's Alaska Journals. Reproduced with permission of the John Muir Center for Regional Studies at the University of the Pacific, Stockton, CA. Courtesy of the Holt-Atherton Department of Special Collections, University of the Pacific Libraries.

played.[9] This was my first general view of Glacier bay—a stern solitude of ice and snow and raw, newborn rocks, dim, dreary, mysterious.

I held my high ground, gained at such cost, for an hour or two, sheltering myself as best I could from the blast, while with benumbed fingers I sketched what I could see of the stormy landscape, and wrote a few lines in my notebook. Then I beat my way back over the snow-smothered ridges and bowlder piles and mud beds, arriving about dark.

Mr. Young told me that the Indians were discouraged and would like to turn back. They feared that I had fallen, or would fall, or in some way the expedition would come to grief in case I persisted in going farther. They had been asking him what possible motive I could have in climbing mountains in such miserable weather and when he replied that I was seeking knowledge, Toyette remarked that Muir must be a witch to seek knowledge in such a place.

After coffee and hard-tack, while we crouched in the rain around a dull fire of fossil wood, the Indians again talked dolefully, in tones that accorded well with the growling torrents about us and the wind among

9. Muir saw the Geikie, Hugh Miller, Grand Pacific, Rendu, and Carroll glaciers.

the rocks and bergs telling sad stories of crushed canoes, hunters lost in snowstorms, etc. Toyette said that he seemed to be sailing his canoe in to a "skookum house" (jail) from which there was no escape, while the Hoonah guide said bluntly that if I was going near the noses of the ice-mountains he would not go with me, for we would all be lost by bergs rising from the bottom, as many of his tribe had been. They seemed to be sinking deeper into dismal dumps with every howl of the storm, when I reminded them that storms did not last forever, and the sun would rise again; that with me they need fear nothing, because good luck followed me always, though for many years I had wandered in higher mountains than these, and in far wilder storms; that Heaven cared for us and guided us more than we knew, etc. This small speech did good. With smiling reassurance Kadechan said that he liked to travel with fearless people and dignified Toyette declared he would venture on, for my "wa-wa was delait" (my talk was very good).

We urged our way against ice and weather to the extreme head of the bay and around it, going up one side and down the other and succeeded in reaching all the main glaciers excepting those at the head of the frozen inlets.

Next to the Muir, the largest of the glaciers enters the bay at its extreme northwestern extension. Its broad, majestic current, fed by unnumbered tributaries, is divided at the front by an island, and from its long, blue wall the icebergs plunge and roar in one eternal storm, sounding on day and night, winter and summer, and from century to century.[10] Five or six glaciers of the first class discharge into the bay, the number varying as the several outlets of the ice fields are regarded as distinct glaciers, or one. About an equal number of the second class descend with broad imposing currents to the level of the bay without entering it to discharge bergs while the tributaries of these and the smaller glaciers are innumerable.

The clouds cleared away on the morning of the 27th, and we had glorious views of the ice-rivers pouring down from their spacious fountains on either hand, and of the grand assemblage of mountains immaculate in their robes of new snow, and bathed and transfigured in the most impressively lovely sunrise light I ever beheld. Memorable, too,

10. The Grand Pacific Glacier, which in 1879 would have been overriding Russell Island. It has since retreated nearly 20 miles up Tarr Inlet.

was the starry splendor of a night spent on the east side of the bay, in front of the two large glaciers north of the Muir. Venus seemed half as big as the moon, while the berg-covered bay, glowing and sparkling with responsive light, seemed another sky of equal glory. Shortly after three o'clock in the morning I climbed the dividing ridge between the two glaciers [the Carroll and Rendu (?)], 2,000 feet above camp, for the sake of the night views and how great was the enjoyment in the solemn silence between those two radiant skies no words may tell.

That morning we had to break a way for the canoe through a sheet of ice half a mile wide, which had formed during the night. The weather holding clear, we obtained telling views of the vast expanse of the Muir glacier and made many sketches. Then fearing that we might be frozen in for the winter we hurried away back through Icy strait into Lynn canal.

Alaska Gold Mines

Returning from his Glacier Bay discovery trip, Muir and his companions visited the coastal regions of present day Haines, Juneau, and "Sum Dum Bay" (Holkham Bay), arriving back at Fort Wrangel on November 20. "The mountains are locked for the winter, and canoe excursions are no longer safe," he wrote in his journal. "Will shut myself in [my] room and work and work."[1] Here he settled into the slow, wet, rainy season by writing up notes and composing at least two Bulletin articles.

In the following letter, mailed just days before Christmas and his departure for California, he summed up what he had learned about the region's gold mines and mining, providing us with a rare and interesting account of early Alaskan gold-mining efforts. It seems a strange topic for Muir, who had passed his earlier days in California looking for "plant gold" and pointedly criticizing those who chased after mineral wealth. The many cheerless descriptions Muir included in the letter concerning mining conditions in the wilderness suggest that he may be trying to discourage viewing wilderness as a mere source for material gain.

Sitka, December 23, 1879[2]

The gold of Alaska is still in the ground, all save a few thousand ounces gathered here and there from the more accessible veins and gravel-beds of the islands and the mountains along the coast. But the cause of the seeming barrenness of the rocks of this northern region is not far to seek, for in the first place, even the coast mountains

1. *Journal*, October 14–December, 1879, *John Muir Papers*, 00029, p. 55.
2. "Alaska Gold Fields," *Daily Evening Bulletin*, Jan. 10, 1880, p. 4, col. 1. There is no

have not been explored to any appreciable extent. Probably not one vein or placer in a thousand has yet been touched by the prospector's pick, while the interior region is still a virgin wilderness—all its mineral wealth about as darkly hidden as when it was covered by the ice-mantle of the glacial period. But light sooner or later is sure to come. Thousands of sturdy miners, graduating from the ledges and gulches of California and Nevada, will push their way over the whole territory and make it tell its wealth. What the developments are likely to be we can only guess. For in our present state of knowledge of the ways of gold, the quantity contained in any formation, however laboriously explored by the geologist, can never be surely counted. We have reason, however, to warrant the opinion that Alaska will be found at least moderately rich in the precious metals, and that gold-mining, notwithstanding the disadvantages of climate, heavy vegetation and beds of glacial drift, will come to be regarded as one of the most important and reliable of her resources.

British Columbia has already yielded gold to the value of about $45,000,000. The Fraser river mines are still productive and profitable, notwithstanding the high price of provisions and all kinds of supplies. The shallow placers have been worked out, but the deep deposits, in old channels similar to the dead river gravels of California, are found to be very rich and extensive. One claim on Lightning creek, which flows into a branch of the Fraser, has yielded over half a million dollars. Other claims in the Cariboo district have proved nearly as rich. Extensive deposits are also being worked on the headwaters of the Columbia, to the northward, and on Peace river.

But the most interesting of the discoveries made hereabouts, as being nearest to the Alaska boundary, and showing the continuity of the

---

trace of this article in *Travels in Alaska*. We do not reprint a subsequent article, his last of the 1879 trip, entitled "Alaska Rivers. Their Number and Characteristics," *Daily Evening Bulletin,* January 20, 1880, p. 4, cols. 3–4. It is largely about rivers and areas outside southeast Alaska and is very close to the *Travels in Alaska* version. For more about John Muir and Alaskan gold, see Buske, "John Muir and the Alaska Gold Rush," and Bruce Merrell, "A Wild, Discouraging Mess: John Muir Reports on the Klondike Gold Rush," *Alaska History*, 7:2 (Fall 1992), pp. 30–39.

gold belt in its northern extension, are in the Cassiar mines, in latitude 59 degrees nearly, on the Dease, Thibert, Defot, McDames's and other creeks, affluent of the great Mackenzie.[3] The placers on these streams would be considered rich even by old Californians, yielding at first from about twenty to a hundred dollars per day to the hand. I visited this region last summer and spent a few days about the mines and on the mountains in the neighborhood. The western margin of the district, as far as it is known, lies at a distance of about a hundred miles from the highest tributaries of the Yukon, and about three hundred from Wrangel, by way of the Stickeen River and Dease Lake. The whole region is heavily overlaid with glacial drift, and there are but few spots even in the beds of the swiftest streams where bedrock is exposed, so that prospecting is carried on under a great disadvantage. Most of the gold samples shown me are quite coarse, and must have been derived from the adjacent rocks. I saw one nugget that weighs forty ounces, several others about half as large.[4] Specimens like beach gravel are common. About 500 to 1000 men have been at work during the last five years fighting for fortune against enormous disadvantages. In the first place, it is a long way up here from California or Oregon, and if the miner waits the opening of the Stickeen to take the steamer to the head of navigation he will not get to work before some time in June. Should he go up on the ice in February or March he would have to drag a load on a hand-sleigh, perhaps assisted by dogs, but it is weary work at the best, making his way through the snow, often breaking through into the ice water, and enduring storm winds that sweep down the cañon from the polar region with a temperature of from 40 to 60 degrees below zero. Arrived at his claim he finds that the spring floods have washed away or filled up ditches, wing-dams, excavations, etc., and he has to begin anew, while the water freezes in the boxes in September, and he has to make haste to get away, or go into winter quarters in a hut to hibernate with the marmots. On the sunless sides of the valleys the ground remains permanently frozen, and all kinds of bread material [food] costs from five to ten times as much as in California mines. Should he go off prospecting on the partial exhaus-

3. At the headwaters of the Stikine River, in British Columbia.

4. By 1915, when *Travels in Alaska* was published—and in all subsequent editions of the book—this remarkable nugget had grown to forty *pounds*. (The largest nugget ever found in Alaska weighed six and one-half pounds; it was discovered in 1901 near Nome.)

tion of his claim, the small summer is done before he can go far or do much. Then his bones begin to ache, and the summer of his life wastes away ere he is aware of the loss.

From what I saw of the mines here I think they are practically exhausted, though perhaps less than one ounce of gold in fifty has been drawn from the deposits worked. But the difficulty is, that under the circumstances the auriferous gravel along the streams mentioned above lies in most places too deep to be profitably worked, while no new discoveries of importance have been made lately. I noticed a good many of the miners standing about, smothered in weary, hangdog meditation, a sure sign of financial distress. The merchants, too, are evidently taking in sail as fast as possible, getting ready to retreat, collecting debts, and paying out as little as they can. Even the saloon-keepers seem discouraged, and ready for flight. These fields, however, will not be wholly abandoned for many years to come. The thrifty and skillful Chinese will work on and make money in deserted claims, while new discoveries will in all probability be made, although the prospects are not encouraging. Two experienced miners set out from Cassiar last spring with a train of pack Indians, and spent the summer in prospecting towards the Yukon without success. Placer mines were discovered on Pelly River, a branch of the Yukon, several years ago.[5]

Turning attention to developments made in Alaska, we find that the most noteworthy of the placers yet discovered in the Territory are located on a glacial stream on the mainland, about 75 miles up the coast from Wrangel, at a place called "Schuck."[6] Thirty or forty miners are said to have made fair wages here for a year or two. These mines are still being profitably worked. The coast region of southeastern Alaska has the advantage of a mild climate—so mild that gold-washing and prospecting may be carried on nearly all winter, while water is everywhere abundant, and provisions cheap.

5. Minor discoveries would continue to be made on the tributaries of the Yukon for many years, culminating in the great Klondike strike of 1896.

6. "Chuck Camp" was located at the mouth of the "Chuck" of "Shuck" river, which flows into Windham Bay, midway between Petersburg and Juneau. (In the Chinook jargon used up and down the Northwest coast at this time, "chuck" meant "water.") The camp, which Muir also described in his letter of August 22, 1880 (see later in this volume), existed only a short time.

On my return voyage in a canoe from the glaciers of Lynn Canal and Cross Sound last November, I met a party of twelve miners in Holkham Bay, who had discovered gold on the outlet of one of the glaciers, and were building a cabin, intending to remain there during the winter. How bright their prospects were they were unwilling to tell.[7] Small quantities have also been washed from the Nass, Stickeen, Taku, and Chilkat rivers, and the "color" of the gold may be found in every stream of considerable size in the Territory, as far as they have been examined.

I have just returned from a visit to a quartz ledge on Baranoff Island, about nine miles from here, and only from one to two miles from deep tide water. It is being vigorously tested by the owners, the Alaska Gold and Silver Mining Company, and is attracting much attention. A ten-stamp mill has been running for a few weeks, and the returns thus far, though not very exciting, are decidedly good. The vein is from about three to four feet wide, exposed on a steep hillside, and will be easily worked all year. The rock taken out from three different levels on the ledge is said to yield on the average from $10 to $15 a ton. The supply of rock seems practically inexhaustible. The mine is particularly interesting as being the northmost of its kind on the gold belt, and, for aught I know, on the continent. We hear also of promising quartz from other portions of Baranoff Island, and from near Tongas, Prince of Wales Island, and several along the Coast Mountains.[8]

The Chilkat Indians have hitherto been hostile to miners entering their country, but last summer one of their chiefs made a formal contract with parties in Wrangel to conduct them on a prospecting tour next spring to the reputed gold mines at the head of the Chilkat river. This outline sketch will, I think, give fair idea of the present condition of mining prospects in the territory. The outlook seems to me neither bright nor dark. Many good gold mines will undoubtedly be discovered here, but nothing in sight will be likely to lead to the conclusion that the richest portion of our gold belt lies in the territory that is nearest the north pole.

7. Holkham Bay, also called Sum Dum Bay in these writings, was thoroughly explored by Muir the following year. His descriptions of that trip are reprinted later in the letter dated August 22, 1880. For a history of mining in Holkham Bay, see Patricia Roppel, "Sumdum," *Alaska Journal*, 1:3 (Summer 1981), pp. 47–50.

8. This is one of the earliest mentions of lode mining in Alaska. The mine was near Sitka at Silver Bay, now the site of a huge, controversial pulp mill.

New Mexico, Arizona, Utah, Nevada, Idaho, Montana and Dakota are more promising fields for the prospector. The climate is generally more favorable, the deposits of gold and other minerals perhaps richer, and more of the rocks are bare and exposed to view like the leaves of a book. I am not seeking to discourage enterprise in this direction. I could not if even so disposed. For Nature, who puts wings on seeds and sends them abroad, also controls the right distribution of men. But there is in some minds a tendency towards wrong love of the marvelous and mysterious, which leads to the belief that whatever is remote must be better than what is near.

The same notion that urges people into the most inaccessible wilderness as the best for fortune-seeking, causes them to look for the richest rocks far below the surface. But throughout the entire gold belt, what is now the surface of the ground, was a short geological time ago from half a mile to a mile below the surface. The mechanical action of the ice during the glacial period degraded the mountains and valleys to this extent at least, so that the exposed edge of a vein is that portion of the vein which before the glacial period could be reached only by making a shaft thousands of feet deep. Let the prospectors then bear in mind that every vein is already sunk on, prospected by Nature herself to a depth of thousands of feet, and therefore that sinking a few feet farther will not be likely to develop anything differing much from what is near the surface. A quartz vein that will not pay near the surface is not likely to pay far below it.

The Trip of 1880

Return to
Fort Wrangel

Muir prolonged his northwest stay through January, 1880, spending that month visiting one of the Fort Wrangel missionaries then living in Portland, where he also gave several lectures on Alaska. Reports on these talks appeared in the local paper, and newspapers throughout the country began to reprint his Bulletin *articles.*

Muir returned to Martinez, California, sometime in February. There must have been some agreement between the bride and groom that John would continue his Alaska travels after their marriage. Not long after the pair moved into the home presented them by her parents, Muir accepted an invitation from John Vanderbilt, the Fort Wrangel merchant with whom he had stayed the year before: "Now you must come up this summer and spend the season with us," Vanderbilt wrote the week following the marriage, "we will take good care of you."[1] Muir returned to Alaska on July 30, telling Louie he would not be back before October.

On the 10th of August Muir was back in Sitka, writing Louie that "I'm about as far north from you as I will be this year—only this wee sail to the North and then to thee, lassie. And I'm not away at all, you know, for only they who do not love may ever be apart." Muir's joy in once again traveling the northern territory is everywhere evident in his writings. While returning to Fort Wrangel, for example, he witnessed the amazing Aurora Borealis and told his new bride, "it was so rare and so beautiful and exciting to us that we gazed and shouted like children at a show."[2]

He disembarked at Fort Wrangel on August 8. Young was waiting, and in a later recollection wrote that Muir "sprinted ashore" to ask, "When can you be ready?"

"Aren't you a little fast," Young replied, "What does this mean? Where's your wife?"

1. John Vanderbilt to Muir, April 20, 1880, *John Muir Papers*, 00909.
2. Badè, ed., *Life and Letters*, II, pp. 150, 155, respectively.

"Man," Muir exclaimed, "have you forgotten? Don't you know we lost a glacier last fall? . . . Get your canoe and crew and let us be off."[3]

Plans had already been drawn up for the return trip to Glacier and Sum Dum bays. Muir wrote again to Louie from Young's home, where he was staying until the upcoming voyage: "I am back in my old quarters, and how familiar it all seems!— the lovely water, the islands, the Indians with their baskets and blankets and berries . . . . Now, my dear wife, the California *will soon be sailing southward, and I must again bid you good-bye. [P.S.] 6 P.M. I have just dashed off a short* Bulletin *letter."*[4] *That letter is reproduced below.*

Of particular interest in this short letter is Muir's sketch of the area's gold mines and his reference to the opening of what later became the famous Yukon gold fields. This Yukon territory had been visited in May of that year by a number of miners from Sitka, who had asked Captain Beardslee to get Indian permission for them to cross on the Chilkoot Trail. Beardslee agreed, insisting that the miners stay together and promise not to supply liquor to the Indians. Nineteen men departed Sitka on May 20th with a detachment of armed sailors from Beardslee's ship, Jamestown. *The Chilkat chiefs were persuaded (or perhaps threatened by the sailors' "Gatling" gun) to permit the miners to use the great pass. Muir, in the following letter, first records how these miners hiked over what would, in 1897, become known as the famous "Chilkoot Pass" trail to the great Klondike fields. These first miners, incidentally, had some small successes in finding gold, and all apparently returned to tidewater areas by the following winter. Muir encountered them later in the month (see his letter of October 7).*

Fort Wrangel, Alaska. August 14, 1880[5]

I am back in my old quarters here, that I left last December, and kindly and familiar everything hereabout seems. The glassy water; the lovely evergreen islands; the Indians with their canoes and their baskets and blankets and berries; the jet ravens, prying and flying about the streets and spruce trees, and the bland, hushed atmosphere brooding tenderly overall.

3. Young, *Alaska Days with John Muir*, p. 126.
4. Badè, ed., *Life and Letters*, II, pp. 150 ff.
5. "Some Alaska Notes," *Daily Evening Bulletin*, August 25, 1880, p. 3, col. 9.

We arrived here early on the morning of the 8th of this month [August, 1880] by the steamer *California*, and the noise of our cannon and whistle was barely sufficient to awaken the sleepy town. The morning shout of one good rooster was the first, and only evidence of life and health that we could get in all the place. Fort Wrangel is very dull at present from a business point of view. The Cassiar gold mines, on which its chief dependence is laid, are being rapidly exhausted; and though the civil war that was in progress when I left here last winter is ended, as well as the later war between the Hootchenoos and Stickines, much of the Indian trade in furs has been driven away, thus greatly increasing the depression due to the failing of the mines.[6]

On the 19th [9th] we arrived at Sitka, and here too, business matters seemed dull, though far less so than in Wrangel. The stoppage of the quartz mill belonging to the Alaska Gold and Silver Mining Company, owing to unfavorable results obtained from a very few month's trial, has of course greatly lessened the activity prevailing here last December. It is hoped that a larger mill will be built, that will enable the Company to work the low-grade rock of the Stewart mine at a fair profit. Prospecting is still being vigorously pushed among the adjacent mountains. One miner, Mr. Halsey, is said to be making good wages by crushing quartz in a large iron mortar. This rock, it is claimed, yields about $400 gold per ton.

The *Jamestown*, lying here, makes, of course, some little stir in the business of the place. Commander Beardslee is evidently a man of conscience, and doing the best he can with the limited means he has for both whites and Indians, and the interests of the Territory in general. With Major Morris,[7] special agent of the Treasury Department, he intended setting out today on the steamer *Favorite* on a cruise through the island waters to the north of here, to look after Government interests among the different tribes of Indians that inhabit this region. The Fort Simpson Indians, it seems, are actively engaged in smuggling British goods into this portion of the Territory, and carrying away large quantities of valuable furs; also the Hoona Indians about Cross Sound complain that

6. Muir was saddened to learn that his Indian companion Toyatte was one of the victims of the war between the Taku faction and the Wrangell Indians, having been shot dead while trying to act as a mediator.

7. William Gouverneur Morris (1832–84) was collector of customs for Alaska at Sitka in the early 1880s.

those same smugglers are killing their sea otters. Last spring a party of 27 miners went through the Chilcat country over the Chilcat divide to the headwaters of the Yukon. They have not been heard from. The party was accompanied by a number of marines from the *Jamestown*, and thus had a good send-off under the wing of the Government. This, I believe, is the first party of whites that the war-like Chilcats have allowed to pass through their country.

On our return from Sitka the *California* called at Klamack [Klawock], a fishing and trading station on Prince of Wales Island, for freight in the shape of canned salmon, fish oil, furs, etc. This station is located on a beautiful bay closely embosomed in the green woods—the one general bay being made up of many smaller ones, each of which would make a charming picture—lovely reaches of glassy water, a margin of yellow-green sedges and bushes, then beveled walls of spruces circling about them in beautiful lines, and snow-capped mountains in the background. How beautiful it all seems in the sunlight, and how beautiful in the stillness of the night with the spangling stars reflected in the waters.

The *California* is about to leave, and this short letter must thus abruptly be brought to a close. I have hired a crew of Stickine Indians, and will set out northward on the 16th in a canoe to study the glaciers and forests.

Revisiting Last Year's Explorations

Ten months separated the time Muir left Alaska for California in 1879, and the day he stepped ashore again at Fort Wrangel. He was in a hurry to start his second canoe voyage, and wrote his wife: "Mr. Young and I have just concluded a bargain with the Indians, Lot and his friend, to take us in his canoe for a month or six weeks, at the rate of sixty dollars per month. Our company will be those two Indians, and Mr. Young and myself, also an Indian boy that Mr. Young is to take to his parents at Chilkat. . . . Tomorrow is Sunday, so we shall not get away before Monday, [August] the 16th. I am trying to trust that you will be patient and happy, and have that work done that we talked of."[1]

In the following articles Muir charts his return up the southeastern waters with Young and the Indians, and a dog named Stickeen, on a one-month voyage of discovery. Throughout, he invites us to reconstruct in our imagination the area as it looked when covered with Ice Age glaciers. He describes the Indian use of blankets as currency, and notes the unfortunate furs-for-molasses (and, through later distilling, furs-for-rum) trade between Indians and Fort Wrangel businessmen. Muir does not care for the squalid look of the Hoonas he meets, and here echoes earlier prejudices about Indian cultures. Yet, in contrast to his descriptions of the Miwok and "Digger" Yosemite Indians, and his comments about the Indians he first encountered at Fort Wrangel the year before, he continues to rethink his views. In this letter he ultimately judges the Alaskan Indians "industrious and honest." He would come to admire them still more, as he continued his adventures.

1. Badè, ed., *Life and Letters*, II, p. 156. The "work" remains obscure. Louie was pregnant at the time and gave birth to a baby girl the following March. The Indians were Lot Tyeen, Hunter Joe, and Smart Billy.

The first Bulletin *article he composed during the return canoe trip is reprinted below. It ranks among the best of his wilderness journalism. Muir paints an alluring picture of the colorful, noiseless,* wildness *of one special campsite, inviting us to join him in the ecstatic chase of wilderness adventure.*

In Camp, Near Cape Fanshaw. August 18, 1880[2]

How delightful it is, and it makes one's pulses bound to get back again into the heart of this grand old northland wilderness, with its giant mountains, glaciers, forests, cataracts, its maze of canals and fiords glowing with sun spangles, and its life-giving air without dust or taint, scented only by the pitch and gum of the woods, and kelp and dulse of the sea. How truly wild it is, and how joyously one's heart responds to the welcome it gives. Drifting along the shores of its networks of channels, we may travel thousands of miles without seeing any mark of man, save at long intervals some little Indian village or faint smoke of a camp fire in some sheltered cove. But even these are confined to the shore. Back a few yards from the beach we are among bushes, with not a leaf out of place, and on forest carpets of moss as trackless as the sky, while the mountains far above the forests, wrapt in their snow and ice and clouds, seem never before to have been even looked at.

Alaska is full of food for man and beast, body and soul, though few are seeking it as yet. Were one-tenth part of the attractions that this country has to offer made known to the world, thousands would come every year, and not a few of them would stay and make homes. At present, however, Alaska is out of sight, though by no means so far and inaccessible as most people seem to suppose. The *California*, a good, well-appointed little steamer of some 700 tons burthen, makes twelve trips a year to Fort Wrangel and Sitka, leaving Portland [Oregon] on the 1st of every month, the actual sailing time between the last-named points being only about five days.

---

2. "Alaska Land," *Daily Evening Bulletin*, September 25, 1880, p. 4, cols. 6–8. Parts of this narrative were rewritten for *Travels in Alaska*, Part II.

The magnificent glacial scenery to the north and east of Sitka is also brought within easy reach by the reliable little steamer *Favorite*, belonging to the Northwestern Trading Company. She sails once a month, or oftener, from Sitka, going as far north as the mouths of the Chilcat and Chilcoot rivers. By this way tourists may obtain views of the celebrated Alaska icebergs that all the world has heard of, and so few even of those who have visited the country have ever seen.

But for those who really care to come into hearty contact with the country, making a long, crooked voyage in a canoe with Indians is by far the better way. The larger canoes made by the Indians will carry from one to three tons, rise lightly over any waves likely to be met on these inland channels, go well under sail, and are easily paddled along shore in calm water or against moderate winds, while snug harbors, where they may ride at anchor or be pulled up on a smooth beach, are to be found almost everywhere. With plenty of provisions in rubber or canvas bags, you may be truly independent, and enter into partnership with nature; to be carried with the winds and currents, accept the noble invitation offered all along your way to enter the sublime rock portals of the mountain fiords, the homes of the waterfalls and the glaciers, and encamp every night in fresh, leafy coves, carpeted with flower-enammelled mosses, beneath wide outspreading branches of the evergreens, accommodations compared with which the best to be found in artificial palaces are truly vulgar and mean.

I left Fort Wrangel on the 16th of this month, accompanied by Mr. [S. Hall] Young, who is a missionary, and also a man, in a cedar canoe about 25 feet long and 5 wide, carrying two small square sails, and manned by two Stickine Indians and a halfbreed. The day was calm and bright, while fleecy clouds, filled with sunshine, hung about the lowest of the mountain brows, while far above the clouds the peaks were seen in the deep blue sky stretching grandly away to right and left in rows and clusters, rising rugged and dark out of broad, waving fields of ice and snow, and shining in as calm a light as that which was falling on the glassy waters beneath them. Our Indians seemed to welcome the work that lay before them, dipping with hearty good will, while we glided past island after island across the delta of the Stickine into Souchoi channel.

By noon we came in sight of a fleet of ice-bergs, coming into Souchoi

Channel [Dry Strait] from a glacier [the LeConte] that flows into the head of a magnificent Yosemite fiord, about twenty miles to the northwest of the mouth of the Stickine river. This is the southmost, as far as I have observed, of the glaciers of the Pacific Coast that flow directly into the sea and send off bergs. It is well known to the Indians, who glide about among the bergs in the smallest of their canoes to hunt seals, though not at all to the whites about Fort Wrangel, though living year after year within less than a day's distance to it. I discovered it last year by tracing the bergs that I found in the open channel up through the narrow high-walled fiord to their sources, making my way for a distance of a least twelve miles through water fairly crowded with bergs, much against the will of our Indians, who feared that their canoe would be broken. The Indian name of this icy field is Hutli, or Thunder Bay, from the sound made by the bergs in falling and rising from the snout of the inflowing glacier.

We floated happily on over the shining water, the mountains of the mainland on our right, Mitgoff [Mitkof], Kuprianoff [Kupreanof], and innumerable smaller nameless islands on our left. Salmon were seen here and there, leaping three or four feet into the air, showing their silvery sides for a moment, then falling with a plash and leaving a mark of foam-bells and widening circles of wavelets. Flocks of gulls, some of them snowy white, slowly winnowed the air overhead, or alighted about the canoe, their smooth breast just touching the water. Ducks, too, of many species were very abundant, rising again and again as we approached, and keeping well ahead of us, or merely diving until we had passed them. The beauty of these islands, appearing in ever-changing pictures as we advanced, were an unfailing source of enjoyment; but chiefly our attention was turned upon the mountains whence all our blessings flow. Now a series of bold granite headlands would fix the eye, or some peak of surpassing grandeur or beauty of sculpture, or some one of the larger glaciers seen exactly in front, its gigantic arms and fingers clasping entire groups of peaks, and its huge trunk sweeping to the sea between huge gray domes and ridges, breaking here and there into shattered cascades, with the azure light filling the crevices and making the most dangerous and inaccessible portion of the glacier the most beautiful of all. Amid such pictures and lessons as these our first day wore away. About sunset the Indians set our tent beneath a Menzies [Sitka] spruce at the mouth of a glacier stream, and spread our blankets on moss two feet deep. The length of the day's sail being about forty miles.

Next morning we sailed around an outcurving bank of boulders and sand ten miles long, that is shoved forward in the channel, and about half exposed at low tide. This curved embankment, of which Point Vanderpent [Vandeput] is the most prominent portion, is the terminal moraine, of a grand old glacier that was at least ten miles wide, and united with the ice-sheet that formerly filled all the channels along the coast. It is located just opposite three large converging glaciers, which formerly united to form the vanished trunk of the glacier to which the moraine under consideration belonged. Because we happened along here in our canoe a few centuries too late, we have missed the grandest feature in the landscape. Enough is left, however, of this noble old ice river, to enable us to restore it by means of the imagination, and see it again about as vividly as if present in the flesh, with snowclouds crawling about its fountains, the sunshine sparkling on its broad, undulating bosom, and its lofty ten-mile ice-wall planted in the deep waters of the channel and sending off its bergs with loud, resounding thunder, night and day, winter and summer, at the rate of one every two or three minutes.

About noon we rounded Cape Fanshaw, scudding swiftly on before a fine breeze, to the delight of our Indians who had now only to steer and chat. Here we came up with two Hoona Indians and their families, who, as they informed us, had been to Fort Wrangel to trade. They had exchanged five sea otter furs, worth about a hundred dollars apiece, and a considerable number of fur-seal, land otter, marten, beaver and other furs and skins, some $800 worth, for a new canoe valued at $80, a few barrels of molasses for the manufacture of rum, provisions, tobacco, blankets, etc.; the blankets not to wear but to keep as money, for the almighty dollar of these tribes is a blanket. The wind died away soon after we met, and as the two canoes glided slowly side by side, the Hoonas made very minute inquiries as to who we were and what we were doing so far north.

Mr. Young's object in meeting the Indians as a missionary they could in part understand, but mine in searching for rocks and glaciers seemed wholly past comprehension, and they asked our Indians whether gold mines might not be the main object. They remembered, however, that I had visited their ice-mountains, as they call the glaciers, at Cross Sound a year ago, and seemed to think there might be, after all, some mysterious medicine interest in them of which they were ignorant. Toward the middle of the afternoon, they engaged our crew in a race, with three paddles against our three oars. We pushed a little away ahead for a time, but though possessing a considerable advantage, as it would seem, in our long oars, they at length overtook us and kept up until after dark, when we camped here together in the rain among tall dripping grass and bushes, some twenty-five miles beyond Cape Fanshaw.

These cold Northern waters are at times about as brilliantly phosphorescent as those of the warm South, and so they were last night in the rain and darkness, with the temperature of the water at 49° Fahrenheit, the air 51°. Every stroke of the oar made a vivid surge of white light, and the canoes left a shining track that faded back into the cold gloom.

As we neared the mouth of the salmon stream, where we intended making our camp, we noticed jets and flashes of silvery light caused by the startled movements of the salmon that were on their way up the stream to spawn. These became more and more numerous and exciting, and our Indians shouted joyfully: *"Hi yu salmon! Hi yu salmon! Hi yu muck-a-muck!"* while the water about the canoe and beneath the canoe was churned by a thousand fins into silver fire.

After landing two of our men to commence camp work, Mr. Young and myself went with our other Indian, Tyeen, a few yards up the stream in the canoe to the foot of a brawling rapid, to see him capture a few salmon. The water everywhere seemed to be literally filled with them, and as they darted in frightened manner to right and left, we appeared to be sailing in boiling, seething silver, marvelously relieved in the jet darkness. Amid the play of these silver waves, and the specially vivid flashes made by the fish darting straight ahead, and the surges made by their doubling suddenly with bent tails, our attention was fixed for a moment by a long, steady, comet-like blaze moving directly toward us from the black, shadowy bank of the stream. On it came, over the salmon and through their midst, intensifying the general auroral glow. But when the portentous object reached the canoe it proved to be only our dog—a very small cause of a very big effect.[3]

3. The dog is Stickeen. This swim was later highlighted in Muir's book *Stickeen* (Boston: Houghton Mifflin, 1909), one of the most popular of all his works. "How eloquent he became" Muir wrote of the dog after the pair had escaped almost certain death from

After getting the canoe into a tide eddy, at the foot of the rapids, Tyeen caught half a dozen salmon in a few minutes, by means of a large hook fastened to the end of a pole. They were so abundant that he simply groped for them in a random way, or aimed at them by the light they themselves furnished. That a skillful Indian can thus procure in a single hour sufficient food to last a month, is a striking illustration of the marvelous fruitfulness of these Alaskan waters.

This morning we found out how beautiful a nook we had got into. Besides the charming picturesqueness of its lines, the colors about it are varied and bright in the rain and exquisitely interblended, making a fine study for a painter.

Our camp-fire smoke is lying motionless in the branches of the trees like a stranded cloud. The Hoonas are up and stirring, the women and children drying their rags and tending the babies, the two men getting firewood and catching salmon. Down on the beach ducks and sandpipers in flocks of hundreds are getting their breakfast, while whales and porpoises are plunging and blowing outside, and great numbers of bald eagles are seen perched on dead spars along the edge of the woods, heavy-looking and overfed, gazing like gorged vultures.

Our Hoona friends, camped at a distance 15 or 20 feet from us, were asleep this morning at sunrise, the whole eight lying together in a heap, wet and limp, like dead salmon. A little boy about six years old, with no other covering than a remnant of a shirt that hardly reached below his shoulders, was lying peacefully on his back, like Tam O'Shanter, despising wind, and rain and fire.[4] His brown, bulging abdomen all the more firmly bent on account of the curvature of the ground beneath him, heaving against the rainy sky, bare as a glacial dome, the rain running down from top of it all around and keeping it as wet as a bowlder on the beach. He is up now, looking happy, and strong and fresh, with

---

a glacier's crevasse, "a perfect poet of misery, and triumphant joy! He rushed round and round in crazy whirls of joy, rolled over and over, bounded against my face, shrieked and yelled as if trying to say, 'Saved, saved, saved!' " Muir's notes about the dog and his adventure appear in Wolfe, *John of the Mountains*, pp. 275–80). Muir's story highlights his adventure on the Taylor Glacier, which he explored later in this 1880 trip.

4. Muir was quoting from the poem "Tam o' Shanter" by his favorite poet, fellow Scotsman Robert Burns.

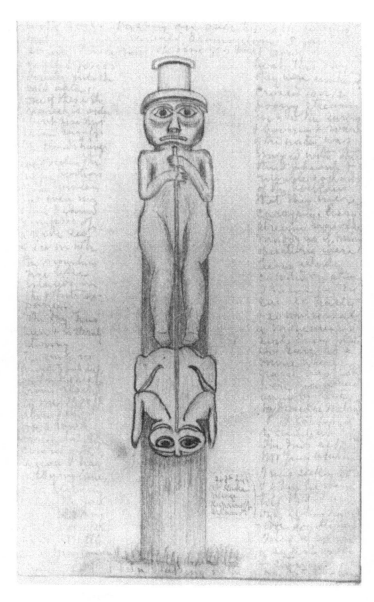

"Totem Pole" (1879), with inscription "20 ft high on Kake Village. Kuprenoff [sic.] Island." Found between pp. 17–18 in John Muir Notebook 00029 (1879 Oct. 14–Dec.). Courtesy of the Holt-Atherton Department of Special Collections, University of the Pacific Libraries.

72

no clothes to dry, and no need of washing while this weather lasts. The two babies are firmly strapped on a board, leaving only their heads and hands free. Their mothers are nursing them, holding the boards on end, while they sit on the ground with their breasts level with the little prisoners' mouths. One of them, a vigorous chubby little fellow, is holding the long, pendulous, cylindrical breast in both fists, and mumbling at the end of it as if he were eating a sausage. They all seem wretched in their wet rags; nevertheless they are strong and well provided for, while, as regards habits of industry, politeness and nice sense of honor they are, perhaps, the equals of the workers of any civilized nation.

As for the salmon, as seen this morning urging their way up the swift, brawling current—tens of thousands of them, side by side, with their backs out of water in shallow places—nothing that I could write may possibly give anything like a fair conception of the extravagance of their numbers. There is more salmon apparently, bulk for bulk, than water. In fording the stream the writhing multitudes, crowding against one another, could not get out of one's way. One of our men waded out in the midst of them and amused himself by seizing them above the tail and swinging them over his head. Thousands of them could thus be taken by hand while they are making their way over the shallows among the stones.

Whatever may be said of other resources of the Territory, it is hardly possible to exaggerate the importance of her fisheries. Not to mention cod, herring, halibut, etc., there are probably not less than a thousand salmon streams in southeastern Alaska, as large or larger than this one (about 40 feet wide) crowded with fine salmon every year. The run commenced this year more than a month ago, and the King Salmon, one of the five species recognized by the Indians, was running the Chilcat river, about the middle of last November.

There are no wheat fields in Alaska, nevertheless, compared with the most fertile portions of all our foodful country, it is pre-eminently the land of plenty.

A Canoe Voyage Among the Islands and Icebergs

Sum Dum, called Holkham Bay on modern maps, lies some 45 miles south of Juneau. It has two forks: Endicott Arm to the southeast, with its northward extension, Fords Terror, and Tracy Arm to the northeast. The extremities of both arms of the bay are now under the protection of the Wilderness System as the "Tracy Arm–Fords Terror Wilderness" and are regularly visited by tourist boats from Juneau and Petersburg.

One century ago, however, both Tracy Arm and Endicott Arm were virtually unknown to the outside world, having been visited only by miners and occasional Indian hunting parties. They did not appear on Vancouver's map from the 1790s, and the 1879 preliminary visit by Muir and Young was the first recorded encounter with the inlet. The entrance to the Bay and some of the miners he met are the subjects of this letter. The mining operations in Holkham Bay were also a topic in Muir's letter of January 10, 1880, reprinted earlier in this volume.

Sum Dum Bay, Alaska, August 22, 1880[1]

On the 18th, after giving our Hoona friends a little tobacco and rice for the purpose of keeping up "Klosh tumtum," (kindly feelings), and taking a long last look at the salmon army in its frantic excelsior march up the rapids, we glided northward along the coast beneath a black, dripping rain-cloud that cut off all the mountains from

1. "Alaska Land," *Daily Evening Bulletin*, October 7, 1880, p. 1, col. 1.

74

sight above 200 feet from the water, and allowed only the base of Admiralty Island to be seen on our left, looking intensely blue in the distance across Prince Frederick's Sound [Frederick Sound]. After rowing a few miles we passed a cluster of picturesque islands at the mouth of Shuck's inlet, or "Shough," as the Indians call it [the Chuck River]. Passing the two imposing headlands that stand guard at the entrance, we proceeded to explore it, though we knew by the purity of the water and the absence of bergs that it contained no great low-descending glaciers, however numerous the smaller ones might be lying in the upper hollows along the mountain walls.

We found it to be about nine miles long, and less than a mile in average width. The walls are from 1,200 feet to 2,000 feet high, rising abruptly out of deep water in beautiful curves clad with a dense growth of feathery spruces to the very top—the narrowest and the greenest of the glacial fiords we had yet seen. On the way up the clouds melted into white sun-filled mist and drifted slowly about the walls in fleecy masses, some of these drawn out into thin, lustrous gauze, through which the trees were plainly seem, producing a most beautiful effect.

About half a mile back from the head of this fall, in a filled-up glacier lake basin, are located the Shough gold mines, which, from the date of their discovery some four years ago, have yielded about $10,000, having been worked in the most primitive way by rockers under great disadvantages. The amount of gold-bearing gravel seems well-nigh inexhaustible; and now that a tunnel has been driven through the rim of the basin to drain it and a good flume built, it is beginning to pay well, though the heavy timber, with its network of interlacing roots covering the deposit, is a great drawback in working it. About a dozen men are employed by the company of three who now own most of the paying claims. These are the first placer mines of any importance that have been discovered and worked in the [Alaskan] Territory; those of the Stickeen river and the Cassiar district being in British Columbia. New diggings have been discovered this summer a few miles from here that are said to pay from $10 to $20 per day to the hand. How extensive this rich deposit may be I could not learn. It is probably quite limited, else large numbers of miners would be already flocking to it.

After climbing alongside the fall and back into the mines by a rough, boggy trail, we retraced our way down the fiord and pushed northward up Stephens Passage, arriving at the mouth of the great Sum Dum Bay at dark on the evening of the 18th, and encamped as best we could on a strip of beach, sand and kelp, hardly above tide water.

The entrance to the main bay is about six miles wide and not very imposing, for though the headlands at the mouth are four or five thousand feet high, they are well timbered and rise in easy slopes without presenting anything extraordinary in their sculpture. The same may be said of the shores on both sides. The icebergs, however, at once attract our admiring gaze. A few large ones are seen drifting about outside in the open passage, and the whole bay is dotted with them, while around the shores of four small islands near the mouth, and along the moraine dam that belonged to a grand old vanished glacier that once filled the entire bay, and around the shores of the bay itself are rows of stranded bergs of every conceivable shape, glittering in the sunlight, and seeming strangely out of place along the edge of the lofty evergreen forest.

Immediately in front as you enter, above the head of the main bay, a large glacier [Sumdum Glacier] is seen pouring its broad crystal flood through the woods down to within 500 feet of the level of the sea, with several smaller ones in deep hollows on either side of it. Then away to right and left stretch two magnificent ice-filled arms, 20 and 25 miles long respectively, reverberating with waterfalls, and containing four glaciers that descend below sea-level and are the sources of the innumerable bergs that fill the bay and its branches. The right arm [Tracy] is scarce at all seen from the main bay, and no hint is perceptible of the surpassing grandeur and beauty of either.[2]

At the foot of the glacier that shows itself so well as we enter from Stephens Passage are located the Sum Dum gold mines. The red, metamorphic slates and quartz that have been ground and are being ground in the glacier mill is the source of the gold, while the foaming torrent that issues from the snout of the glacier is used in washing it from the moraine gravel and mud. Even the Indians, not much given to studies

---

2. Here and in the letter of August 19th, Muir confuses an understanding of the geography of the area by his use of "right" and "left." It seems certain that his "right" arm is Tracy Arm, and his "left" arm is Endicott Arm, with its tributary named Fords Terror.

of this sort, recognize the action of the ice in this connection. "That glacier up there is digging the gold for those fellows," said one of our crew, as he ceased rowing for a moment and gazed thoughtfully on the grand spectacle. Almost as soon as you enter the bay you hear the roar of the torrent belonging to the gold mine glacier in making its way through the woods, and leaping into the bay in a showy cataract.

Half a mile to the west of the fall there is a small Indian village belonging to the Sum Dum tribe, numbering thirty-seven, all told. They subsist chiefly on salmon and seals, the latter found among the icebergs, mostly well up the two long arms of the bay, near the snouts of the glaciers. They are busily engaged now drying and smoking their winter supply of salmon, which gives their little town quite a lively aspect. This is one of the brightest and warmest of Alaskan days, and there is no lack of life to enjoy it. Ducks and gulls in large flocks are flying about or resting on the smooth water. Plovers throng the beach, with here and there a kingfisher and ouzel, while eagles, well filled with fish, are taking their ease, riding on icebergs or perched motionless on the tops of dead poles. The principal sounds are the thunder of breaking bergs left in strained positions by the receding tide, the swash and plapping of small waves under the projecting bases of those that are afloat, the scream of the eagle, rattle of the kingfisher, the pleasant voices of the many species of gulls and ducks, and the sustained roar of the cataract.

The mines here were discovered last fall by a party of prospectors from Fort Wrangel. Since that time they have built substantial cabins and made a good beginning. Some ten are at work. They told me that the mines were not rich, but that since provisions were readily obtainable at a low price they could make fair wages when the water was not too high, say from $2 to $5 a day.

This evening I met six of the party of prospectors that went up a branch of the Chilkoot river and over the divide among tributaries of the Yukon. They are now on their way back to Fort Wrangel, prospecting along the coast as they go. They report that though placers were found in several places, none of those were rich enough to pay so remote from any reliable base of supplies. They had no difficulty with Indians; on the contrary, they were extremely well treated by them. The Yukon region through which they passed is mostly plain or gently undulating, covered with grass and patches of small pines. The soil, they said, seemed to them rich enough and the climate warm enough for good crops of wheat and barley.[3]

Some little prospecting has also been done this summer about Cross Sound, and a few claims have been located. The quartz ledges on Baranoff Island are still receiving a good deal of attention, and promise well. The Stewart lode, on which work has been suspended, is still considered valuable property by the owners, the Alaska Gold and Silver Mining Company. The Superintendent tells me that the Company, having already spent a good deal of money on their mine, hesitate as to whether they had better build a large mill and develop the mine or sell it to a New York Company who wish to buy it. This Company, the Superintendent tells me, has offered $150,000 for the mine. They have purchased the Henriette claim, on the same lode, and several others, and expect to have a thirty-stamp mill on their property by the 1st of January.[4]

Reviewing Alaska mines in general, I see nothing to change the conclusions arrived at last year, while discussing the subject in the *Bulletin*, that this country will be found moderately rich in the precious metals, but owing to obstacles in the way of their development, all the other resources—fish, furs, timber, etc.,—will be brought into the markets of the world long before any considerable quantity of mineral wealth has been uncovered.

3. These were some of the miners who had trekked the Chilkoot trail the previous year, after Captain Beardslee had convinced Indians to let them use the pass.

4. This claim was located five miles south of Sitka. The Superintendent was George Pilz, who later hired Richard Harris and Joseph Juneau to look for gold on the mainland east of Sitka. On October 3, 1880, the pair made the first major gold discovery of any magnitude in Alaska, which would result in the founding of the city of Juneau. See R. N. DeArmond, *The Founding of Juneau* (Juneau: Gastineau Channel Centennial Association, 1967), pp. 33–51.

Exploring Endicott Arm

The first object of the 1880 trip was to investigate Sum Dum Bay and explore its glaciers, and in particular find the "lost glacier" that the party had seen the year before but could not then approach.

Muir was giving himself only one month of Alaska, so there was some sense of urgency as the group launched this trip. Muir wished to travel fast: "Our canoe was light and easily propelled," Young remembered of this second journey. "Our outfit was very simple, for this was to be a quick voyage and there were not to be so many missionary visits this time. It was principally a voyage of discovery; we were in search of the glacier that we had lost."[1]

Their first five days of sailing and paddling had brought the group past Cape Fanshaw to "Shuck's Inlet" (see Muir's letters earlier) and finally to their objective, Sum Dum Bay. They entered the night of August 18: "Here we were to find the lost glacier," Young wrote of this part of the trip. "This deep fiord has two great prongs. Neither of them figured in Vancouver's chart, and so far as records go we were the first to enter and follow to its end the longest of these, Endicott Arm." The next few days found the group exploring the Endicott, extending southeast from the opening of Holkham Bay, and the "lost" glacier that Muir named for Young. That grand glacier, at the farthest end of the bay, is no longer called the "Young," and modern visitors must look for the "Dawes" glacier. "Some ambitious young ensign on a survey vessel, perhaps, stole my glacier," Young wrote later, "and later charts give it the name Dawes. I have not found in the Alaskan statute books any penalty attached to the crime of stealing a glacier, but certainly it ought to be ranked as a felony of the first magnitude, the grandest of grand larcenies."[2]

    1. This and the following comments by Young are from *Alaska Days With John Muir*, pp. 136–37, 140–41, and 147, respectively.

    2. The U.S. Coast and Geodetic Survey renamed the glacier in 1891, after Henry Dawes, a Massachusetts lawyer and statesman.

Cascade Camp. Sum Dum Bay, August 19, 1880[3]

This morning one of my good times came after a year's waiting, for then I set out under a happy group of welcoming conditions to explore the long left arm [Endicott] of this icy bay, with everything to bring glacial success. I was here last year during a stormy time, towards the end of November, when, after urging my way through the ice for fifteen miles, I was compelled to turn back by stress of weather and the danger of being frozen in.

We got away from camp about 6 o'clock, and pulled merrily on through fog and rain along the beautiful wooded shore on our right, passing bergs here and there, the largest of which, though not over 200 feet long, seemed, as they loomed gray and indistinct through the fog, to be at least half a mile long, and 100 feet high. For the first five hours the sailing was open and easy, nor was there anything very exciting to be seen or heard, save now and then the thunder of a falling berg rolled and echoed from cliff to cliff, and the sustained roar and white outbounding arches of cascade among the cliffs.

About 11 o'clock we reached a point where the fiord presented an unbroken front of packed ice all the way across, and we ran ashore to fit a block of wood on the cutwater of our canoe to prevent its being battered or broken. While Tyeen, who had considerable experience among berg-ice, was at work on the canoe, the other Indians prepared a warm lunch, making a fire with wood that had been collected by the Sum Dum Indians.

The smooth, sheltered hollow where we landed seems to be a favorite camping ground of those Indians in coming and going to hunt seals. The pole-frames of tents, tied with cedar bark, are left standing on level spots, while the ground about them is strewn with seal bones and bits of salmon and spruce bark. I also noticed several sweat-houses and a number of square frames, made of crossed splints of cedar, tied at the points of inter-

---

3. "Alaska Land. An Eventful Day," *Daily Evening Bulletin*, October 9, 1880, p. 4, col. 1.

section with strips of bark. These are used, the Indians tell me, for the purpose of drying sections of the thick bark of the Merten spruce [Western hemlock] on, to prepare it for winter use as food. Large quantities of this astringent are eaten, after being soaked in hot water, by the Indians hereabouts, in connection with their greasy seal and fish, for food. I saw large numbers of trees that had thus been cut down and peeled along the shores of Chatham Strait, Lynn Canal, Prince Frederic [Frederick] Sound and elsewhere.

For a mile or two we found the work of pushing through the ice rather tiresome. An opening of twenty or thirty yards would be found here and there, then a close pack that had to be opened by pushing the smaller bergs aside with poles. I enjoyed the labor, however, for the fine lessons I got, and in an hour or two we found zigzag lanes of water, through which we paddled with but little interruption, and had leisure to study the wonderful variety of forms the bergs presented as we glided past them. The largest we saw did not greatly exceed 200 feet in length, or twenty-five or thirty feet in height above the water. Such bergs would draw from 150 to 200 feet of water. All those that have floated long undisturbed have a projecting base at the water line, caused by the more rapid melting of the immersed portion. When a portion of the berg breaks off, another base line is formed, and the old one, sharply cut, may be seen rising at all angles, giving it a marked character, while many of the oldest ones are beautifully ridged by the melting out of angular furrows running strictly parallel from side to side, revealing the bedded structure of the ice, acquired centuries ago, far back on the mountain whence it came. A berg suddenly going to pieces is a grand sight, especially when the water is calm. Then there is no visible motion, save perchance the slow drift in the tide current, and the prolonged roar of its fall comes with startling effect, and heavy swells are raised to tell what has taken place, and tens of thousands of its neighbors rock and swash in sympathy, repeating the news over and over again. We were too near several large ones that fell as we passed, and our canoe had narrow escapes. The Indians in pursuit of seals are frequently killed in this manner.

In the afternoon, while we were admiring the scenery, which, as we approached the head of the fiord, becomes more and more sublime, one of our Indians called attention to a flock of wild goats on the mountain side overhead, and soon afterwards we saw two other flocks, at a height

Camp with tent and fire. From Muir's Alaska Journals. Reproduced with permission of the John Muir Center for Regional Studies at the University of the Pacific, Stockton, CA. Courtesy of the Holt-Atherton Department of Special Collections, University of the Pacific Libraries.

of about 1,500 feet, relieved against the mountain as white spots. They are very abundant here and throughout the Alaskan Alps in general, feeding on the grassy slopes above the timber line, in company with the wild sheep.[4] Their long, yellowish hair is shed at this time of year, and they are now snowy white. None of nature's cattle are better fed or better protected from the cold. Tyeen told us that before the introduction of guns they used to hunt them with their wolf-dogs, and thus bringing them to bay among the rocks, where they were easily approached and killed.

The upper half of the fiord is about a mile to a mile and a half wide, and shut in by sublime Yosemite cliffs, nobly sculptured, and adorned with snowy falls, and cascades, and fringes of trees, and bushes and small patches of flowers. The general interest grows as we advance, but amid so crowded a display of novel beauty it is not easy to concentrate the

4. The mountain goat, *Oreamnos americanus*, is common on Southeast Alaska's mainland. Muir's "wild sheep" is presumably the Dall sheep, *Ovis dalli dalli*, whose range overlaps that of the mountain goat only in Southcentral Alaska, near Anchorage.

"Left side of the grand tributary, S.D." [Sum Dum Bay]. Note canoe in foreground, left. From Muir's Alaska Journals. Reproduced with permission of the John Muir Center for Regional Studies at the University of the Pacific, Stockton, CA. Courtesy of the Holt-Atherton Department of Special Collections, University of the Pacific Libraries.

attention long enough on any portion of it without giving more days and years than our lives can afford. I was determined, at least, to see the grand fountain of all this ice. As we passed headland after headland, hoping as each was rounded we should obtain a view of it, it still remained very perfectly hidden. "Ice mountain hi yu Kumtucks hide," said Tyeen, (glaciers know how to hide extremely well,) as he rested for a moment after rounding a huge granite shoulder of the wall, whence we expected to gain a view of the extreme head of the fiord. The bergs, however, towards the head were nowhere closely packed and we made good progress, and finally found our game occupying a branch of the fiord that comes in from the northeast, at half-past 8 o'clock, 14 1/2 hours after setting out.

The [Dawes] glacier is about 3/4ths of a mile wide at the snout, and probably about 800 feet deep, with a wall of beautifully carved ice about 150 feet high facing the deep blue water of the fiord. It is much wider a few miles farther back, the snout being jammed between sheer granite walls from 3,500 to 4,000 feet high. It shows grandly from where it broke on our sight, as it comes sweeping boldly forward and downward in its majestic channel, swaying from side to side around stern unflinching rock pillars in graceful fluent lines. While I stood in the canoe making a sketch of it several bergs came off with a tremendous dash and thunder, raising a fine dust and spray of ice and water to a height of 100 feet. "The ice mountain is well disposed toward you" said Tyeen. "See, he is firing his big guns to welcome you."

After completing my sketch and entering a few notes I directed the Indians to pull around a lofty burnished rock on the west side of the channel, where, as I knew from the trend of the canyon, a large glacier once came in, and what was my delight to discover that this glacier was still in existence, and still pouring its ice in the form of bergs into a branch of the fiord. Even the Indians shared my joy and shouted with me. I expected only one first class glacier here, and found two. They are only about two miles apart, and how glorious a mansion does that precious pair dwell in! After sunset we made haste to seek a camp ground. I would fain have shared these upper chambers with the two glaciers, but there was no landing in sight, and we had to make our way a few miles in the twilight to the mouth of the side-cañon, where some timber was seen on the way up. There seemed to be a good landing as we approached the shore, but coming nearer we found that the granite fell directly into deep water without leaving any level margin, though the slope a short distance back is not very steep.

After narrowly scanning the various seams and steps that roughened the granite, we concluded to attempt a landing rather than grope our way further down the fiord through the ice. And what a time we had climbing on hands and knees up the slippery rocks to this little garden shelf some 200 feet above the water, and dragging indispensables after us. But it is a glorious camp after all, the very best of the trip. For in the first place, it is set in a charming little garden, with the flowers in bloom, and ripe berries are nodding from a fringe of bushes around its edges, and close alongside, to the right of us, there is a lofty mountain capped with ice, and from the blue down-curved edge of that ice-cap there are sixteen silvery cascades, all in a row, falling about 4,000 feet, each one of the sixteen large enough to be heard at least two miles.

How beautiful is the fire-light on the nearest larkspurs and geraniums and daisies of our garden! How hearty the wave-greeting on the rocks below, sent us by the two glaciers! And how glorious a song the sixteen cascades are singing!

Shooting the Rapids

Finding the "lost glacier" put Muir and the group into the best of spirits. After a dinner of mallard duck, biscuits and coffee, Muir told his friend Young, "Ah! What a Lord's mercy it is that we lost this glacier last fall, when we were pressed for time, to find it again in these glorious days. . . . My Friend, we are the richest men in all the world tonight."

Exploring the furthest reach of Endicott, the group next turned their canoe toward the "Yosemite branch" of the main fiord. Entrance into the arm at first proved impossible. Icebergs blocked the path, and the tremendous tidal action coming from this Yosemite arm forced the group to wait until the following morning to attempt a second entrance.

"There is your Yosemite," Muir said to Young when the pair at last gained a view of the glacial valley, "only this one is on a grander scale. We'll call this Yosemite Bay—a bigger Yosemite, as Alaska is bigger than California."[1]

Muir's elation is everywhere evident in the account of the six-hour visit to Alaska's "Yosemite" that follows.

---

1. These two quotations are from Young, *Alaska Days with John Muir,* pp. 154, 157, respectively. Muir's name for the hidden valley did not last. It was renamed in 1889 for Harry L. Ford, a member of a Navy survey party. See R. N. DeArmond, *Southeast Alaska Names and How They Got There* (Juneau: privately published, 1989), pp. 33–34 for the history of names in Holkham Bay.

Gold Camp, Sum Dum Bay. Alaska, August 20, 1880[2]

The song of our sixteen cascades made us sleep all the sounder last night, and we were so happy as to find this morning that the bergs and berg-waves had spared our canoe, and that our way down the fiord was comparatively open. Sliding ourselves and our baggage down the rocks we set off in high spirits down the fiord and across to the right side to explore a remarkable branch of the main fiord [Fords Terror] that I had noted on the way up, and that, from the magnitude of the glacial character of its advertisement on the two colossal rocks that guard our entrance, promised a rich reward for our pains.

After we had sailed about three miles up this narrow side fiord we came to what seemed to be the head of it, for trees and rocks swept in a curve around from one side to the other without showing any opening, although the walls of the canyon were seen extending back indefinitely, one majestic brow beyond the other, into the alps.

In tracing this curve, however, in a leisurely way, in search of a good landing, we were startled by Captain Tyeen shouting "Skookum chuck! Skookum chuck!" (strong water, strong water) and found our canoe being carried sideways by a powerful current, the roar of which we had mistaken for that of a big waterfall. We barely escaped being swept over a rocky bar on the boiling, foaming flood, which, as we afterwards learned, would have been only a happy push on our way. After we had effected a landing we climbed the highest rock near the shore to seek a view of the channel beyond the rapids, to find out whether or no[t] we could safely venture in.

Up, over rolling, mossy, bushy, burnished rock we dragged and scrambled for an hour or two, which resulted in a fair view of the deep blue waters of the fiord stretching on and on along the feet of the most majestic Yosemite rocks we had yet seen. This determined our plan of

2. "Alaska Land. Perilous Adventure—Shooting the Rapids," *Daily Evening Bulletin*, October 16, 1880, p. 4, col. 3.

shooting the rapids and exploring it to its fartherest recesses. This novel interruption of the channel is caused by a bar of exceedingly hard granite, over which the great glacier that once occupied it swept, without degrading it to the general level, and over which the tide-waters now rush in and out with the violence of a mountain torrent in the spring time, when the snow is melting.

Returning to the canoe, we pushed off, and in a few moments were racing over the bar with lightning speed through leaping waves, and swirling eddies, and sheets of rock-dashed foam; our little shell of a boat tossed and twirled as lightly as a bubble. Then rowing across a belt of back-flowing water, we found ourselves gliding calmly along a smooth mirror reach between granite walls of the very wildest and most exciting description conceivable. Altogether, there is nothing in the far-famed Yosemite Valley that will compare with it in impressive, awe-inspiring grandeur.

As we drifted silent and awe-stricken beneath the shadows of the mighty walls which, in their tremendous height and abruptness seemed to overhang at the top, the Indians gazing intently, as if they, too, were impressed with the strange grandeur that shut them in, at length broke silence by saying, "This must be a fine place for woodchucks [marmots?]." When I asked them, further on, how this gorge was made, they gave up the question, but offered an opinion as to the formation of rain and soil. The rain, they said, was produced by the rapid whirling of the earth by a stout mythical being called Yek.[3] The water of the ocean was thus thrown off, to descend again in showers, just as it is thrown off a wet grindstone. They did not, however, understand why the ocean water should be salt, while the rain from it is fresh. The soil, they said, for the plants to grow on is formed by the washing of the rain on the rocks and gradually accumulating. The grinding action of ice in this connection they had not recognized.

Gliding on and on, the scenery seemed at every turn to become more lavishly fruitful in forms as well as more sublime in dimensions. Snowy falls booming and blooming in splendid dress, colossal domes and battlements, and sculptured arches of a fine neutral gray tint, all laved by the

---

3. *Yek* are the spiritual helpers of the Tlingit shaman. See Aldona Jonaitis, *Art of the Northern Tlingit* (Seattle: University of Washington Press, 1986), p. 26.

deep blue water; green ferny dells, bits of lower bloom on ledges, fringes of willow and birch, and glaciers above all. But when we approached the base of a majestic rock, like the Yosemite Half-Dome, standing at the head of the fiord where two short branches put out, and came in sight of another grand glacier of the first order, sending off bergs, our joy was complete. I had a most glorious view of it. Sweeping in grand ease and majesty from the deep inaccessible mountains where its fountains are laid, swaying around one mighty bastion after another, until at length it falls into the fiord in shattered overleaning fragments, which, when set free, become bergs, and so waste again to water, and die in the sea. When we had feasted awhile on this unhoped-for treasure, I directed the Indians to pull to the head of the left fork of the fiord, where we found a large cascade, with a volume of water great enough to be called a river, but no more great glaciers.

This is in form and origin a typical Yosemite Valley, though as yet its floor is covered with ice and water—ice above and beneath. How noble a mansion in which to spend a winter and a summer! It is about ten miles long, and from three-quarters of a mile to one mile wide. It contains ten large falls and cascades, the finest one on the left side near the head. After coming in an admirable rush over a granite brow where it is first seen at a height of 900 or 1,000 feet, it leaps a sheer precipice of about 250 feet, then divides and reaches the tide-water in broken rapids over bowlders. Another, about 1,000 feet high, drops at once onto the margin of the glacier two miles back from the snout. Several of the others are upwards of 3,000 feet high, descending through narrow gorges as richly feathered with ferns as any channel that water ever flowed in, though tremendously abrupt and deep. A grander array of rocks and waterfalls I have never yet beheld.

The amount of timber on the walls is about the same as that on the Yosemite walls, but owing to greater moisture there is more small vegetation—bushes, mosses, grasses, etc.; though by far the greater portion of the area of the wall surface is bare, and shining with the polish it received when occupied by the glacier that formed the entire cañon. The deep-green patches seen on the side of the mountains back of the walls at the limit of vegetation are grass, where wild goats, or chamois rather, roam and feed. The still greener and more luxuriant patches farther down in gullies and slopes where the declivity is not excessive, are made up mostly of willows, birch and huckleberry bushes, with a varying amount of prickly ribes, and rubus, and echinopanax. This growth when approached, especially on the lower slopes near the level of the sea at the jaws of the great side cañons, is found to be the most impenetrable and tedious combination of fighting bushes that the weary explorer ever fell into, incomparably more punishing than the buckthorn and manzanita tangles of the Sierra.

The cliff gardens of this hidden Yosemite are exceedingly rich and beautiful. On almost every rift and bench, however small, as well as on the wider table-rocks where a little soil had lodged, we find companies of fine bright flowers, always fresh, and also far more brilliantly colored than would be looked for in so cool and beclouded a region—larkspurs, geraniums, painted-cups, blue-bells, gentians, sedums, saxifraxes, epilobiums, violets, parnassia, veratrum, orchids, fritilaria, smilax, spiranthus, asters, daisies, the yellow pond lily, bryanthus, cassiope, linnea, and a great variety of flowering ribes and rubus and heathworts. Many of the above, though with soft bush stems and leaves are yet as brightly painted as those of the warm sunlands of the south. The heathworts in particular, are very abundant and beautiful, both in flower and fruit, making delicate green carpets for the rocks, flushed with pink bells, or dotted with red and blue berries. The grasses are everywhere tall, with ribbon leaves well tempered and arched, and with no lack of bristly spikes, and nodding purple panicles. The Alpine grasses of the Sierra, making close carpets on the glacier meadows, I have not yet seen in Alaska.

The ferns are less numerous in species than in California, but about equal in the number of fronds. I have seen three Aspidums, two Woodaias, a Lomaria, Polypodium, Cheilanthes and a Pteris.

In the great left or eastern arm of this Sum Dum Bay and its Yosemite branch, I counted from the canoe, on my way up, and down, 30 small glaciers above and back of the walls, and, as we have seen, three of the first order, also 37 cascades and falls, counting only those large enough to make themselves heard four or five miles. The whole bay, with its rocks and woods and ice, reverberates with their roar. How many glaciers may be disclosed in the other great arm that I have not seen as yet, I cannot say, but I guess not less than a hundred pour their turbid streams into the fiord, making about as many joyful, bouncing cataracts.

About noon we began to retrace our way back into the main fiord, and arrived here at the Gold mine camp after dark, rich and weary.

Among the Glaciers, Cascades, and Yosemite Rocks

The following article describes Muir's journey with his three Indians companions up the Tracy Arm of Sum Dum Bay. Here Muir spends, he claims, "two of the brightest and best of all my Alaska days."

Sum Dum Bay, August 29, 1880[1]

I have another fine lot of ice to offer, some thirty-five or forty square miles of bergs, one great glacier of the first-class, descending into the fiord at the head, which is the fountain from whence of all these bergs derived, and thirty-one smaller glaciers that do not reach tide-water; also, nine cascades and falls, large size, and two rows of Yosemite rocks from 3,000 to 3,500 feet high, each row about twenty miles long, burnished and sculptured in the most telling glacial style, and well trimmed with spruce groves and flower gardens; a' that, and twice as muckle as a'that,[2] of a kind that cannot be catalogued, the whole being the result of two days' exploration in the right arm of this noble bay

1. "Alaska Land. Among the Glaciers," *Daily Evening Bulletin*, October 23, 1880, p. 4, col. 1. See also *Travels in Alaska*, pp. 333ff.
2. Muir paraphrases his favorite poet, Robert Burns.

[i.e., the Tracy Arm]. I began this grateful toil yesterday morning, setting out with three Indians, Mr. Young having decided to remain at the gold mine. For the first five or six miles there is nothing very striking in the scenery as compared with that of the outside channels, where all is so evenly beautiful, excepting the multitude of bergs.

The afternoon was wearing away as we pushed on and on through the drifting bergs, without our having obtained a single glimpse of the great king glacier or any of its tributaries. A Sum Dum Indian whom we met groping his way deftly through the ice in a very small canoe, hunting seals, told us that the ice mountain was yet fifteen miles away. This was towards the middle of the afternoon, and I gave up sketching and making notes and worked hard with the Indians to reach it before dark. About 7 o'clock we approached what seemed to be the extreme head of the fiord, and still no king glacier in sight—only a small one, three or four miles long melting a thousand feet above the sea. . . .

At length, towards 9 o'clock, just before the gray darkness of evening fell, a long, triumphant shout told that the glacier [Sawyer Glacier], so deeply and desperately hidden, was at last hunted back to its benmost bore. A short distance round a second bend of the cañon I reached a point where I obtained a good view of it, as it pours its deep, broad flood into the fiord in a majestic course from between the noble mountains, its tributaries, each of which would be regarded elsewhere as a grand glacier, converging from right and left from a fountain set far in the silent fastness of the Alaskan Alps.

"There is your lost friend," said the Indians laughing; "he says *sagh-a-ya*," (how do you do?) And while berg after berg was being born with thundering uproar, they said, "Your friend has *klosh tumtum* (good heart) hear! He is firing his big guns in your honor."

After our successful hunt I waited long enough to make an outline sketch, and then urged the Indians to hasten back some six miles to the mouth of a side canyon I had noted on the way up as a place where we might camp in case we should not find a better. After dark we had to move with great caution through the ice. One of the Indians was stationed in the bow with a long pole to push aside the smaller fragments and look out for the most promising openings through which he guided us, shouting "*Frotay. Tucktay!*" (Shoreward, seaward), about ten times a minute. We reached this landing place about 10 o'clock, guided in the darkness by the roar of a glacier torrent that the canyon carries. The ground is made of angular boulders and it was hard to find a place among them, however small, to lie on. The Indians laid down in the canoe to guard against drifting ice, after assisting me to set my tent in some sort of way among the stones, well back beyond reach of the tide. I asked them as they were returning to the canoe if they were not going to eat something. They answered promptly, "We will sleep now, if your ice will let us. We will eat tomorrow, but we can find some bread for you if you want it." No, I said, go to rest. I too will sleep now and eat tomorrow. Nothing was attempted in the way of light or fire. Camping that night was simply lying down. The boulders seemed to make a fair bed after finding the best place to take their pressure.

During the night I was awakened by the beating of the spent ends of berg-waves against the side of my tent, though I had fancied myself safely high and dry. These special waves are not raised by wind or tide, but are caused wholly by the fall of large bergs from the snout of the glaciers or sometimes by the overturning or breaking of large bergs that may have long floated in perfect poise. The highest of berg-waves often-times travel half a dozen miles or farther before they are much spent. . . .

When the Indians came ashore in the morning and saw the condition of my tent they laughed heartily and said, "Your friend (meaning the big glacier) sent you a good word last night, and his servant knocked at your tent and said, '*Sagh'aya,* are you sleeping well?'"

I had fasted too long to be in very good order for hard work. I made out, however, to push my way up the canyon before breakfast, while the Indians were cooking, to seek the glacier that once came into the fiord, knowing from the size and muddiness of the stream that drains it that it must be quite large and not far off. I came in sight of it after a hard scramble of two hours through thorny chaparral and across steep avalanche taluses of rocks and snow. . . .

Returning, I reached camp at 10 A.M. for breakfast; then had everything packed into the canoe, and set off leisurely across the fiord to the mouth of another wide and low canyon, whose lofty outer cliffs, facing the fiord, are glacial advertisements of a very telling kind. How gladly I should have explored it all, traced the streams of water and streams of ice, and entered its highest chambers, the homes and fountains of the snow. But I have to wait. I only stopped an hour or two, and climbed to the top of a rock through the common underbrush, whence I had a good general view. The snout of the main glacier is not far distant from the fiord, and sends off small bergs into a lake. The walls of its tributary canyons are remarkably jagged and high, cut in a red variegated rock, probably slates. On the way back to the canoe I gathered ripe salmonberries an inch and a half in diameter, ripe huckleberries, too, in great abundance, and several interesting plants I had not before met in the territory.

About noon we set out on the return trip to the Gold-mine camp, the Indians paddling leisurely with the tide through a lavish labrador of bergs. The sun shown free and warm. No wind stirred. The spaces between the bergs were as smooth as glass, reflecting the unclouded sky, and doubling the beauty of the bergs as the sunlight streamed through their innumerable angles in rainbow colors. The thinnest lance-sharp edges were tipped with radiating needles of silver. Soon a light breeze sprang up, and dancing lily spangles on the water mingled their glory of light with that burning on the angles of the ice.

On days like this, true sun days, some of the bergs show a purplish tinge, though most are white from the disintegration of the surfaces exposed to the weather. Now and then one is met that is pure blue crystal throughout, freshly broken from the snout of the fountain glacier, or recently exposed to the air by turning over. But in all of them, old and new, there are azure caves and rifts of ineffable beauty, in which the purest tones of light pulse and shimmer lovely and untainted as anything on the face of the earth.

As we were passing the Indian village I presented a little tobacco to the head men as an expression of regards, while they gave us a few smoked salmon. After putting many questions concerning my exploration of their bay, and bluntly declaring their disbelief in the ice-business.

About 9 o'clock we arrived at the Gold camp, where we found Mr. Young ready to go on with us tomorrow morning, and thus end two of the brightest and best of all my Alaska days.

Taku Inlet:
A Perfect Day

*In the following article, the last written by Muir for the year and the last of our col-
lection, Muir describes a visit to Taku Inlet. He had bypassed the Taku the previous
year, his entrance attempt pushed back by a "violent wind." He now returned, wishing
to explore its upper reaches.*

*Within a month, Muir would be back in California with his wife, and business,
and the "defrauding" duties which awaited his life and career. Seldom again could
he recapture the freedom of this "Perfect Day" in Alaska's Taku Inlet. And so, there
is a sense of closure in this final letter, as Muir concludes the little party had been
"happily rich" during "one of the best of all my Alaska days."*

Mouth of Tahkou River, Alaska, August 24, 1880[1]

I never saw Alaska looking better than it did yesterday, when we bade
farewell to Sum Dum and pushed on northward up the coast toward
Tahkou. The morning was extremely beautiful—clear, calm,
bright—not a cloud in all the purple sky, nor wind, however gentle, to
shake the slender spires of the spruces on the heights or the dew-laden
grass-leaves around the shores. Over the mountains and over the broad
white-bosoms of the glaciers the sunbeams poured, rosy and warm as
ever fell on a field of ripe wheat, drenching the forests and kindling the

1. "Alaska-Land. A Perfect Day," *Daily Evening Bulletin*, November 13, 1880, p. 4, col. 1.
Portions of this letter reappear in *Travels in Alaska*, pp. 234–42.

glassy waters of the bay and the icebergs in a perfect blaze of colored light. Every living thing seemed joyful, and nature's work went on with enthusiastic activity. . . .

No better day could be given to suggest the coming fruitfulness of this ice region, and to show the advance that has been made from glacial winter to fruitful summer. The careful commercial lives we lead hold our eyes away from the operations of God as a workman. Yet they are openly carried on from day to day through unmeasured geological seasons, and all who will look may see.

Our Indians, exhilarated by the fine sunshine that morning, were garrulous as the gulls and plovers, and pulled heartily at their oars, evidently glad to get out of the ice with a whole boat. "Now for Tahkou," they said, as we glided over the shining water. "Good bye Ice Mountains, good bye Sum Dum."

Soon a light breeze came, and they unfurled the sail and laid away their oars and began as usual in such free times to put their goods in order, unpacking and sunning provisions, guns, ropes, clothing, etc. Joe has an old flintlock musket suggestive of Hudson Bay times, which he wished to discharge and reload. So stepping in front of the sail, he fired at a gull that was flying past before I could prevent him, and it fell slowly with outspread wings alongside the canoe, with blood dropping from its bill. I asked him why he had killed the bird, and followed the question by a severe reprimand for his stupid cruelty, to which he could offer no other defense than that he had learned to be careless about taking life from the whites. Tyeen, our Captain, who is a better man, denounced the deed as likely to bring bad luck. Before the whites came among them, most of these Indians held, with [Louis] Agassiz, that animals have souls, and that it was wrong and unlucky to even speak disrespectfully of the fishes or any of the animals that supplied them with food.[2]

A case illustrating their superstitious beliefs in this connection occurred at Fort Wrangel last year while I was there. One of the subchiefs of the Stickines had a little son five or six years old, to whom he was very much attached, always taking him with him in his short canoe trips, and leading him by the hand while going about town. Last sum-

2. Muir here references his own belief in the famous geologist's views.

mer the boy was taken sick, and gradually grew weak and thin, where-upon his father became alarmed, and feared, as is usual in such obscure cases, that the boy had been bewitched. He first applied in his troubles to Dr. Carliss,[3] one of the missionaries, who gave medicine, without effecting the immediate cure that the fond father demanded. He was, to some extent, a believer in the power of missionaries, both as to material and spiritual affairs, but in so serious an exigency it was natural that he should go back to the faith of his fathers. Accordingly, he sent for one of the Shamans, or medicine men, of his tribe, and submitted the case to him, who, after going through the customary incantations, declared that he had discovered the cause of the difficulty. "Your boy," he said, "has lost his soul, and this is the way it happened. He was playing among the stones down on the beach, when he saw a crayfish in the water, and made fun of it, pointing his finger at it and saying, 'Oh, you crooked legs! Oh, you crooked legs! You can't walk straight; you go sideways,' which made the crab so angry that he reached out his long nippers, seized the lad's soul and pulled it out of him and made off with it to deep water. And," continued the medicine man, "unless his stolen soul be restored to him and put back into place he will die. Your boy is really dead already; he only seems to live; it is only his lonely, empty body that is living now, and though it may continue to live in this way for a year or two, the boy will never be of any account, not strong, nor wise nor brave."

The father then inquired whether anything could be done about it; was the soul still in possession of the crab, and if so, could it be recovered and reinstalled in his forlorn son? Yes, the doctor rather thought it might be charmed back and reunited, but the job would be a difficult one, and would probably cost about fifteen blankets.

After we were fairly out of the bay into Stephen's Passage, the wind died away, and the Indians had to take their oars again, which ended our talk. On we sped over the silvery level, close along shore, meeting fresh exciting beauty all the way. . . .

Toward evening we came to a village at the head of a picturesque bay, belonging to the Tahkou tribe. We found it silent and deserted. Not a single lawyer, doctor or policeman had been left to keep it. They are so happily rich as to have but little of a perishable kind to keep, nothing worth fretting about. They were away catching salmon, our Indian said.

3. W. H. R. Corlies, or Corleis, a Baptist missionary in Fort Wrangel.

All the Indian villages hereabouts are thus abandoned at regular periods every year, just as a tent is left for a day, while they repair to fishing, berrying and hunting stations, occupying each in succession for a week or two at a time, coming and going from the main, substantially built villages. Then, after their summer's work is done, the winter supply of salmon dried and packed, fish oil and sea [seal?] oil stored in boxes, berries and spruce bark pressed in cakes, their trading trips completed, and the year's stock of quarrels with the neighboring tribe patched up in some way, they devote themselves to feasting, dancing and hootchenoo drinking. The Tahkous were once a powerful and warlike tribe, but now, like most of the neighboring tribes, they are whiskied nearly out of existence. They have a larger village on the Tahkou river, but, according to the census taken this year by the missionaries, they number only 269 all told—109 men, 79 women and 81 children. The comparative numbers of the men, women and children show the vanishing condition of the tribe at a glance.

Our Indians wanted to camp for the night in one of the deserted houses, but I urged them on into the clean wilderness until dark, when we landed on a rough, rocky beach, fringed with devil's clubs, greatly to the disgust of our crew. We had to make the best of it, however, as it was too dark to go father. After supper was accomplished among the boulders, they retired to the canoe, which they anchored a little way out, beyond low tide, while Mr. Young and I, at the expense of a good deal of scrambling, discovered a spot on which we slept among the thorny panax.

This morning, about two hours after leaving our thorny camp, we rounded a great mountain rock, nearly a mile in height, and entered the Tahkou fiord [Taku Inlet]. It is about 25 miles long, and from 3 to 5 miles wide, and extends directly back into the heart of the Alaskan Alps, draining hundreds of noble glaciers and streams. The ancient glacier that formed it, fed by its tributaries, was far too deep and broad and too little concentrated to erode one of those narrow cañons, usually so impressive in sculpture and architecture, but it is all the more interesting on this account, when the grandeur of the ice work accomplished is seen. This fiord, more than any other that I have examined, explained the formation of that wonderful system of channels extending along the coast from Puget Sound to about latitude 50 degrees, for it is a marked portion of the system—a branch of Stephen's Passage.

And its trends and general sculpture are as distinctly glacial as those
of the narrowest fiord, while many of the largest tributaries of the great
glacier that occupied it are still in existence. I counted some forty-five
altogether, big and little, in sight from the canoe in sailing up the middle of the fiord. Three of them came down to the level of the sea at the
head of the fiord, from a magnificent group of snowy mountains, forming a glorious spectacle as seen from near the head of the channel. The
middle one of the three [Taku Glacier] belongs to the first class, pouring its majestic flood, shattered and crevassed, directly into the fiord,
and crowding about twenty-five square miles of it with bergs. The next
below it [Norris Glacier] also sends off bergs occasionally, though a narrow slip of glacial detritus separates the snout from the tide-water. This
forenoon a large mass fell from the snout damming the outlet, which
at length broke the dam, and the flood that resulted swept forward
thousands of small bergs across the mud-flat into the fiord with tremendous energy. In a short time all was quiet again; the flood-waters receded,
leaving only a large blue scar on the snout and stranded bergs on the
swept moraine flat to tell the tale.

These two magnificent glaciers are about the same size—two miles
wide—and their snouts are only about a mile and a half apart. While
I sat sketching them from a point among the drifting icebergs, where
I could see far back into the heart of their distant fountains, two Tahkou
Indians, father and son, came gliding toward us in an extremely small
canoe. Coming alongside with a good-natured "saghaya," they inquired
who we were, our objects, etc., and gave us information about the river,
their village and two other large glaciers that descend nearly to the sea-
level a few miles up the river cañon [East and West Twin Glaciers.]
Crouching in their little shell of a boat among the great bergs, with paddle
and barbed spear, they formed a picture as arctic and remote from
anything to be found in civilization as ever was sketched for us by the
explorers of the far north.

Making our way through the crowded bergs to the extreme head of
the fiord, we entered the mouth of the river, but were soon compelled
to turn back on account of the strength of the current. The Tahkou is
a large stream, nearly a mile wide at the mouth, and like the Stickine,
Chilcat and Chilcoot, draws it sources from far inland, crossing the
mountain chain from the interior through a majestic canyon, and draining a multitude of glaciers on its way.

The Tahkou Indians, with a keen appreciation of the advantages of their position for trade, hold possession of the river, and compel the Indians of the interior to accept their services as middlemen, instead of allowing them to come down the river to trade directly with the whites.

When we were baffled in our attempt to ascend the river, the day was nearly done, and we began to seek a camp-ground. After sailing two or three miles along the left side of the fiord we were so fortunate as to find a small nook in the rocky wall, described to us by the Tahkou Indians, where firewood may be obtained, and where we could drag our canoe up the bank beyond the reach of the ice. Here we are safe, with a fine outlook over the bergs to the great glaciers, and near enough to have the full benefit of the thunder of the bergs falling from their snouts.

This has been one of the best of all my Alaska days; clear and warm, and full of glacier interest throughout.

The sunset in this glorious mountain mansion, with the weather so perfect, was intensely impressive. After the dark water of the fiord was in shadow, the level sunbeams continued to pour through the square miles of bergs with ravishing beauty, every one of them reflecting and refracting the purple light like cut crystal. Then all save the tips of the highest became dead white. These, too, were speedily quenched, the glowing points vanishing one by one like stars sinking beneath the horizon in a clear frosty night. And after the shadows had crept gradually higher, submerging the glaciers, and the ridges between them, the divine Alpen glow still lingered about their fountains, and the lofty peaks laden with ice and snow stood in glorious array, flushed and transfigured.

Now the last of the twilight purple has vanished, the stars begin to shine, and all trace of the day has gone. Looking across the fiord the water seems perfectly black, and the two great glaciers are seen stretching dim and ghostly back into the mountains, that now are massed in darkness against the sky.

Chronology
Notes on Sources
Index

Chronology

1879

April   *Scribner's Monthly* article by W. H. Bell, "The Stickeen River and Its Glaciers" inspires Muir's trip to Alaska?

9   Muir writes his friend, Jeanne Carr: "The Sunday convention manager offered me a hundred dollars for two lectures on the Yosemite rocks in June. . . I want to spend the greater portion of the season up the Coast, observing ice. . ."

June 2   G. S. Mackey of San Francisco writes Muir with a "promised letter of introduction . . . to the premier of British Columbia" and adds, "I do hope you and Mr. McGee [Magee] will enjoy your visit to the Northern wilderness muchly."

9–11   Sunday school convention in Yosemite Valley; meets Alaska missionary Sheldon Jackson.

19   Writes to friends on the eve of his departure: "Goodbye, I am going home. Going to the mountains, to the ice & forests & flowers." Proposes to Louie Wanda Strentzel at her parents' house in Martinez, California

20   Departs San Francisco for Victoria on the *Dakota* with Thomas Magee and his teenage son, William

24   Arrives Victoria, B.C.; by boat from Victoria to Port Townsend, Washington Territory

25   Port Townsend to Seattle; Seattle to Olympia via Tacoma and Steilacom on the *Zephyr*

26   Returns to Seattle; boards the *Dakota* for Victoria

27   Arrives Victoria

29   Victoria to New Westminster via Nanaimo, on the *Wilson G. Hunt*

30   Arrives New Westminster

July 2 Arrives Yale, head of navigation on the Fraser River; returns to Portland via Victoria and Seattle?

9 Departs Portland on the *California*

10 Writes Louie from Victoria

14 Arrives Fort Wrangel

15–16 In Sitka; writes to friends

17 Arrives Fort Wrangel from Sitka on the *California*

21–23 Abortive Chilkat trip with "divines" on the chartered paddle-wheel steamboat *Cassiar*

22 "Great Glacier day" at Baird Glacier

23 "Deserted Village day" at Old Wrangell

28 First excursion up the Stikine River

31 Climbs Glenora Peak; rescues Young

Aug 1 Returns from Glenora with Young

2 Arrives Fort Wrangel

3 Fort Wrangel Presbyterian church officially organized

5 "Toyatte Entertainment" with Tlingit Indians

12 Sheldon Jackson departs on 250-mile canoe trip to the south

19 Muir ascends the Stikine River to its headwaters; writes Louie from cabin on Thibert Creek near Dease Lake

Sep 18 Visits the "Garnet Glen" near Fort Wrangel

19 S. Hall Young's first child born—Abby Lindsley Young

Oct 5 Fort Wrangel Presbyterian church occupied

9 Writes Louie from Fort Wrangel. Note on October 9 letter to Louie: "Leaving for the north in a few minutes [in a large cedar canoe] Indians waiting Farewell"

14 Young's article from *The Glacier* (April 1886) and Muir's journal say this was the date they left Ft. Wrangel

17–19 Travels along Kupreanof Island

20 Paddles and sails 50 miles around southern tip of Admiralty Island to lower Hootsnehoo village

21 Arrives Killisnoo (near Angoon)

23 Arrives Hoonah

24 Departs Hoonah for Glacier Bay; loads firewood at Pleasant Island; camps at Berg Bay

25 Crosses Glacier Bay to Tlingit hunting camp near Beartrack Cove; re-crosses Bay to Geikie Glacier

26 Sunday (no travel); climbs ridge north of Geikie Inlet

27   Paddles to Hugh Miller Glacier; camps on point to the west of Russell Island at northernmost arm of Glacier Bay

28   Explores ridges near camp

29   Thin ice forming; camps at Tidal Inlet; spends night climbing by starlight north of camp

30   South to Tlingit Point and a view of Muir Glacier; across Glacier Bay to earlier camp at Geikie Inlet; sees Muir Glacier at a distance; out of Glacier Bay to camp on Pleasant Island

Oct 30–Nov 4   En route to "country of the Chilkats" at northern end of Lynn Canal

Nov 4–8   Stays with Tlingits at Hindasetukee (site of today's Haines airport); climbs part way up "the mountain back of the village" (Mount Ripinski)

8   Departs and camps in Bridget Cove, north of Juneau

9   In camp at Bridget Cove (Sunday)

10   Visits Auk village; camps at Fritz Cove

11   Visits fish camp on Douglas Island, and at "three very dirty huts" on mainland (Salmon Creek or Gold Creek?); down Gastineau Channel to camp near Point Bishop

12   South past Taku Inlet and Port Snettisham to Sumdum (Holkham Bay)

13   Explores Endicott Arm

14   Camps at Hobart Bay

15   Camps to north of Cape Fanshaw on Whitney Island

16–17   In camp

18   Around Cape Fanshaw; camps in a "cosy cove"

19   Escapes breakers at Point Vandeput; camps near Point Agassiz

20   Passes LeConte Glacier, camps on island at mouth of the Stikine River

21   Arrives at Fort Wrangel

Nov 21–?   Writing at Fort Wrangel

Dec 23   Letter to the *Daily Evening Bulletin* mailed from Sitka

27   Letter to the *Daily Evening Bulletin* mailed from Sitka

1880

Jan 6   Muir writes fiancée Louie from Portland, Oregon: ". . . will be back on the [*George W.*] *Elder* which leaves this port about the 15th I think."

Jan 6–23? In Portland and Vancouver, Washington giving lectures

Feb ? Returns to San Francisco

Apr 14 Marries Louie Strentzel in Martinez
     20 John Vanderbilt of Ft. Wrangel writes Muir that he "must come up this summer and spend the season with us, we will take good care of you."
     21 John Muir's 42nd birthday

Jun 9 John Vanderbilt writes, ". . . it would afford us the greatest pleasure if you can extend your wedding trip to this section where we would entertain you in sailing about the country."

Jul 1 Thomas Magee writes Muir suggesting an Alaska trip
     15 Magee writes with details on steamers
     30 Departs San Francisco with Magee for Alaska, on the *Dakota*; Louie stays in Martinez

Aug 4 Departs Victoria on the *California*
      8 Arrives Fort Wrangel; S. Hall Young is there
   9–11 On the *California* via Peril Strait to Sitka, writes Louie from Sitka
  12–13 En route to Fort Wrangel, via Klawock, on the *California*
     14 Arrives Fort Wrangel; writes long letter to Louie
     16 Departs Fort Wrangel in canoe with Young, Tlingits, and the dog Stickeen
     19 Explores Endicott Arm of Holkham Bay, camps near its end
     20 Explores the "Yosemite branch" (Fords Terror); returns to Sumdum mining camp
     21 Good weather; at Sumdum
     22 North from Sumdum to deserted Taku village
     23 Enters Taku Inlet
  24–26 Enroute to Glacier Bay
     26 Camps at Taylor Bay
  29–30 Adventure with dog Stickeen on Taylor (Brady) Glacier

Fall 1880 Returns to Sitka via Tenakee Inlet; then via steamer to Fort Wrangel and San Francisco

Notes on Sources

The collected letters in this book were feature stories typical of John Muir's wilderness journalism from the 1870s through the 1890s. Microfilm copies of all his San Francisco *Daily Evening Bulletin* articles may be found at the University of the Pacific (Stockton, CA), the Bancroft Library at the University of California, Berkeley, and the California State Library, Sacramento, California.

The John Muir Center for Regional Studies at the University of the Pacific is the major repository for Muir manuscripts and his other papers. Ronald Limbaugh, Director of the Center, presided over the compilation of the *John Muir Papers* in a microfilm edition; this film includes Muir's Alaskan journals and correspondence as well as drafts of Alaskan articles and books. Over twenty libraries have acquired the Papers on microfilm; these are also available for interlibrary loan from the University of the Pacific. The notes made by biographers William F. Badè and Linnie Marsh Wolfe are also available, as are the Muir/Strentzel Family and Legal Papers, articles, maps, scrapbooks, and memorabilia. Muir's personal library of over 700 volumes, encompassing 509 titles, is a recent addition to the Center's collection.

The most important of Muir's letters and journals were published decades ago and remain significant sources for those interested in studying John Muir's life. The seminal works are William F. Badè, ed., *The Life and Letters of John Muir*, 2 vols. (Boston: Houghton Mifflin Co., 1923–24); and Linnie Marsh Wolfe, ed., *John of the Mountains: The Unpublished Journals of John Muir* (Boston: Houghton Mifflin Co., 1938). These volumes, together with Wolfe's biography, *Son of the Wilderness: The Life of John Muir* (New York: Alfred A. Knopf, 1945), provide a straightforward but uncritical account of Muir's life. The best of the modern biographies include T. H. Watkins, *John Muir's America* (New York: Crown, 1976), the first to look behind the legend; Stephen Fox, *John Muir and His Legacy: The American Conservation Movement* (Boston: Little, Brown, 1981); Michael P. Cohen's passionate and rewarding *The Pathless Way: John Muir and American Wilderness* (Madison: University of Wisconsin Press, 1984); and Frederick Turner's excellent *Rediscovering America: John Muir in His Time and Ours* (New York: Viking, 1985).

Muir's first published newspaper article, "Yosemite Glaciers: The Ice Streams of the Great Valley," which appeared in the New York *Daily Tribune* (December 5, 1871), is reprinted in Robert Engberg and Donald Wesling, eds., *John Muir to Yosemite and Beyond* (Madison: University of Wisconsin Press, 1980). Muir's newspaper letters written immediately after he left Yosemite for travels up and down California, appearing in the San Francisco *Bulletin*, have been collected in Engberg, ed., *John Muir Summering in the Sierra* (Madison: University of Wisconsin Press, 1984). His early articles calling for a halt to timber cutting and sheep herding in the higher Sierra Nevada were "God's First Temples," published in the Sacramento *Record-Union* (February 1876) and "Great Evils From the Destruction of Forests," San Francisco *Real Estate Circular* (April 1879) (the latter was reprinted in *The Pacific Historian* [Winter 1981]). Besides the 1879–80 letters in this present collection, Muir produced a large series of Alaskan letters to the *Bulletin* in 1881, describing events on the Bering Sea along both the Russian and Alaskan coasts; these were edited by Badè and published as *The Cruise of the Corwin* (Boston: Houghton Mifflin Co., 1917). Another small set of Alaskan letters was sent by Muir to *The* [San Francisco] *Examiner* during the Klondike gold rush in 1897.

Muir prepared other Alaska pieces for publication, drawing upon his phenomenal memory and the journals he kept during his travels. These writings are described in detail in William F. and Maymie B. Kimes, *John Muir: A Reading Bibliography* (Fresno: Panorama West Books, 1986), a chronological listing of all known Muir publications, with annotations and a thorough index.

Only one Alaska book by Muir made its way into print while the author was still living. His small volume *Stickeen: The Story of a Dog* (Boston: Houghton Mifflin, 1909) has enjoyed many reprints. Muir's best known Alaskan title, *Travels in Alaska* (Boston: Houghton Mifflin Co., 1915) gives an account of the trips described in this book's collection, plus a narrative of his 1890 experiences in Glacier Bay. Never satisfied, Muir reworked the text of this book many times, and a manuscript lay on his bed, incomplete, when he died in 1914. For more about Muir's place in the history of Glacier Bay see Dave Bohn, *Glacier Bay: The Land and the Silence* (Gustavus, AK: Alaska National Parks and Monuments Association, 1967); and Kim S. Heacox, "Advances and Retreats at Glacier Bay," *Pacific Discovery*, 34:4 (October/December 1983), pp. 4–17.

We are fortunate to have another look at many of Muir's Alaskan adventures through the eyes of S. Hall Young, who accompanied him during most of the events described in the present collection. In his *Alaska Days with John Muir* (New York: Fleming H. Revell Co., 1915), Young embellishes with gusto and manages to resurrect a remarkable quantity of dialogue, decades after the events described. His writing is entertaining and is considered mostly authoritative. His autobiography, *Hall Young of Alaska: "The Mushing Parson"* (New York: Fleming H. Revell, 1927) contains much of interest about southeast Alaska at the time he and Muir explored the region together. ("I feel pretty sure that you should change the name of the book which you say you will call the 'Mushing Parson'," Muir once warned Young. "Mushing is slang, even in Alaska, and parsons should be better described no matter how they travel." [Muir to Young, May 31, 1910].)

Other contemporary accounts of the Alaskan scene include Sheldon Jackson, *Alaska, and Missions on the North Pacific Coast* (New York: Dodd, Mead, 1880); William Gouverneur Morris, *Report on the Customs District, Public Service, and Resources of Alaska Territory* (Washington, D.C.: Government Printing Office, 1879); W. H. Pierce, *Thirteen Years of Travel and Exploration in Alaska, 1877–1889* (Anchorage: Alaska Northwest Publishing Co., 1977), reprint of 1890 edition; and the first tourist guidebook to Alaska, Eliza R. Scidmore's excellent *Alaska: Its Southern Coast and Sitkan Archipelago* (Boston: Lothrop, 1885). For more on the rise of Alaska tourism, see Ted C. Hinckley, "The Inside Passage: A Popular Gilded Age Tour," *Pacific Northwest Quarterly* (April 1965), and Frank Norris, *Gawking at the Midnight Sun* (Anchorage: Alaska Historical Commission, 1985). For old Fort Wrangel, see Clarence Andrews, *Wrangell and the Gold of the Cassiar* (Seattle: Luke Tinker, 1937). A good modern survey of the period is Hinckley, *The Americanization of Alaska, 1867–1897* (Palo Alto: Pacific Books, 1972). Recent work on the Tlingit Indians has been published by Frederica de Laguna, "Tlingit," *Handbook of North American Indians*, vol. 7, *Northwest Coast* (Washington, D.C.: Smithsonian Institution, 1990), pp.. 203–28; and Robert T. Boyd, "Demographic History, 1774–1874," *ibid.*, pp. 135–48. De Laguna has also edited a monumental new book, based on the field notes of George Thornton Emmons, *The Tlingit Indians* (Seattle: University of Washington Press, 1991). It has quickly become the landmark reference work on Tlingit culture.

Two recent collections of essays on Muir include work by Frank E. Buske about the naturalist's years in Alaska: "John Muir and the Alaska Gold Rush," in Lawrence R. Miller and Dan Collins, eds., *The World of John Muir* (Stockton: Holt-Atherton Pacific Center for Western Studies, 1981), pp. 37–49; and "John Muir's Alaska Experience," in Sally M. Miller, ed., *John Muir: Life and Legacy* (Stockton: University of the Pacific for the Holt-Atherton Pacific Center for Western Studies, 1985), pp. 113–123. An important contribution to understanding Muir's view of glaciers is in the same collection; see Paul D. Sheats' "John Muir's Glacial Gospel" (*ibid.*, pp. 42–53). See also Buske's "John Muir: 'Go to Alaska. Go and see.'," *Alaska Journal* (Summer 1979), pp. 32–37; and Jed Dannenbaum, "John Muir and Alaska," *Alaska Journal* (Autumn 1972), pp. 14–20. For a discussion of the literary merits of Muir's Alaskan writings, see Herbert F. Smith, *John Muir* (New Haven: Twayne Publishers, 1965), pp. 101–22. Richard F. Fleck examines Muir's evolving attitude toward Native Americans, with a close look at Alaskan Natives, in *Henry Thoreau and John Muir Among the Indians* (Hamden, CT: Archon Books, 1985), pp. 41–70.

For current news of Muir-related scholarship and events, the *John Muir Newsletter* is published by the John Muir Center for Regional Studies, University of the Pacific, Stockton, CA.

Index